▼ *The Packing Book* ▼

The Packing Book

Secrets of the Carry-on Traveler

Judith Gilford

Ten Speed Press
Berkeley, California

TEN SPEED PRESS
P.O. Box 7123
Berkeley, CA 94707

Cover design by Nancy Austin
Text design by Victor Ichioka
Cover and text illustrations by Richard Sigberman

Library of Congress Cataloging-in-Publication Data
Gilford, Judith
    The packing book : secrets of the carry-on traveler /
by Judith Gilford.
        p.   cm.
    ISBN 0-89815-599-1
    1. Travel.   I. Title.
G151.G54   1994
910'.2'02—dc20   93-50552
                                      CIP

FIRST PRINTING 1994
Printed in the United States of America

    2   3   4   5 — 98   97   96   95   94

Contents

▼ Acknowledgments

Many thanks to the following knowledgeable people and organizations for contributing interviews and materials:

Pamela Bracken, Overseas Adventure Travel (OAT); Bill Dawson, REI Adventure Tours; and David Kalter, Hostelling International/ American Youth Hostels (AYH), for sharing the outstanding packing lists that are used in their adventure travel programs; wardrobe consultants Carol Bell, Joyce Beadle, Linda Curyea, Karen Snow, and Laura Santi; Kevin Reid, Keeble and Schuchat Photography; Keith Taylor, REI; Dick Ellenwood and A.W. Kershaw, The Walk Shop; Bill Meehan, Florentine Luggage; Aris Export; Elliot Wahba and staff, Norm Thompson; Don Rosberg, Norma Beckstead, and Gloria Bertiglia, Westwind; Christopher Dennis, Edwards Luggage; Jeffrey Pfeiffer, MEI; Jeffrey Longbrake, Flexo-Line; Cathryn Hartnett, L. L. Bean; Barbara Starner, Remin Kart-a-Bag; Mike Harrelson, Patagonia; Debbie Licolli and Barry Gevertz, Lullaby Lane; Nancy Gold, Tough Traveler; Sally DeMasi, Wolf Computer; Hank Verbais, FAA Office of Public Affairs; Dee Donaldson, Accent on You; Suzanne Hogsett.

Thanks also to all my family members and friends for their moral support, ideas, information, and babysitting; and especially to Kathleen Keough, Roger Rapoport, Peter Beren, Kai Wessels, George Young, Nancy Austin, Frances Bowles, Victor Ichioka, Sharilyn Hovind, Bruce Lobree, Julie Lavezzo, and the entire staff at Easy Going.

My special thanks to my husband, David, for his love, logic, and unwavering faith; to Nathan and Sara, for their cheerful hugs, patience, and understanding (and help with the kids' section); to my incredible mother, Thelma Elkins, founder of Easy Going, who has been telling me for years that "it oughtta be a book!"; and to my father, Mort Elkins, for his optimism and humor.

Introduction—
Singing the Overpacker's Blues

Welcome to Overpackers Anonymous! If you've ever experienced that sinking feeling while staring at your bed on the night before departure, clothes piled high on it and an open suitcase on the floor, this is the book for you. Perhaps you suffer from the "just-in-case" syndrome, convinced that you have to take every piece of clothing you own on a two-week trip. Do you feel compelled to pack a different outfit for morning, noon, and night? Perhaps you do not do any packing at all, preferring simply to play helpless and let a poor overburdened mate do all the heavy lifting.

Do not worry, you are not alone. In my years of teaching packing seminars at Easy Going Travel Shop and Bookstore in Berkeley, California, and for large corporations, clothing stores, and civic organizations, I have discovered that everyone, even the most seasoned traveler, worries about packing. For good reason. Many victims of the syndrome overcorrect and end up leaving home without some of the essentials they need. If you have ever shopped for intimate apparel in Moscow or a pair of size 13 loafers in Escanaba, you know the feeling.

Another problem is that every trip is different. You have just mastered packing for formal business trips when you decide to take a beach vacation or to go to Europe with the family. Sometimes you go by air, sometimes by car or perhaps by train. Sometimes you do not care how much your bag weighs; at other times it is crucial to travel light if you are to be able to negotiate the trip.

Finding the balance is the key. You really *can* pack everything you need in order to feel comfortable on the road in a single carry-on suitcase. This book is designed to make all travelers feel better about packing by making the process manageable. You will be able to take what you need without weighing yourself down. On the road you'll find packing and unpacking is a snap.

This book covers the basics of trip preparation to make your packing infinitely easier and less painful. It discusses airline regulations and the finer points of luggage, travel-wardrobe planning, fabric selection and care, and travel gear. Plus, it shows you a great technique for packing. *The Packing Book* will be useful no matter what kind of trip you are taking *this time*. "This time" can mean a formal five-day business trip, a family weekend getaway, a week at a beach resort, or a three-week combination work and play vacation in two climates.

▼ Your Traveling Lifestyle and a Flexible Packing Plan

Trips vary in the activities they entail, how mobile you want to be, and the level of choice that you want in your wardrobe and accessories. Some trips require more formal clothing, some are entirely casual. Sometimes you want to be self-sufficient and travel very light. At other times you are willing or want to have a bigger wardrobe and more accessories, even if the trade-off is heavier luggage. Sometimes you want as much variety as possible and will accept heavier luggage and perhaps even two pieces. But do not worry, by using this book, whatever your traveling lifestyle, you'll be able to get there carry-on!

Remember, planning is the essential key to anxiety-free packing. Even if you are not leaving next week, read the background information, so that when you are ready to hit the road, you have put together a versatile wardrobe that you can pack in less time than you would have believed possible.

1 The Carry-on Craze

Let's play travel trivia. Here are three questions for you:

1. How many pieces of luggage are handled by the airlines each year?
2. How many pieces of luggage are lost by the airlines each year?
3. What happens to all that lost luggage?

Now, the answers. The airlines handle more than 600 million pieces of luggage annually. They lose approximately thirty thousand pieces. This is not bad. But where does all that lost luggage end up? In Alabama, according to the *San Jose Mercury News* (Dec. 10, 1989). Apparently, once the airlines have made every effort to find the owners and have failed to do so, the bags and their contents are sold, in wholesale lots, to merchants in Scottsboro, Alabama. Here, the merchandise is displayed in small storefronts and sold, retail, at discount prices.

And that's not all; there's more bad news. According to a recent report in the *Los Angeles Times*, luggage theft by employees is on the rise. In two FBI operations, Grab Bag and Ramp Check, at O'Hare International Airport in Chicago, agents "seized $250,000 worth of goods and cash and filed charges against sixteen airport workers, accusing them of taking jewelry, video equipment, mink coats, cash, and even guns from passengers' bags." The article went on to say that the thieves in Chicago allegedly concentrated on baggage being transferred from one airline to another, because responsibility was difficult to assign. The U.S. attorney in Chicago said that the thieves simply "zipped or ripped bags open, took what they liked, then sent the luggage on its way, some of it 'pretty well torn up.' Stolen goods were often stashed in public areas until the end of the rogue baggage handler's shift. By one account, an airport security guard knowingly helped carry booty to the thief's car." This type of internal theft at major airports is being reported around the country, in addition to the usual thefts from passengers who fail to keep an eye on their luggage in waiting areas.

Obviously the fear of losing their luggage is the main reason that many travelers these days want to carry it on the plane. Also, it is faster: carrying your own luggage allows you to bypass the carousels at the airport and move right on to your destination. Business people are especially taken with carry-on, as they want to get off the plane and get right to their appointments (time is money). Some travelers prefer to be self-sufficient, especially when they are touring many destinations that are off the beaten track. Diverse modes of transportation often create the need to be able to manage luggage without help from porters.

There are times, however, when carry-on luggage is neither necessary nor practical. If you plan to check in your luggage on a nonstop flight; if you require bulky cold-weather clothing or gear; if your health prevents you from handling your own luggage; if your luggage is being handled for you by the tour company; if you are going on a formal business trip and need several suits or dresses; if you are traveling with small children and lots of equipment; if you are going on a cruise that requires several outfits, evening gowns, tuxedoes, and so on; or, if you are in the fashion business and *must* have ten pairs of shoes and sixteen outfits, all unrelated. For the rest of us, my carry-on strategy will simplify life on the road.

This book focuses on carry-on travel because more and more travelers are discovering that carry-on is not only desirable but also feasible for all kinds of trips. The designs and fabrics of carry-on luggage have become very sophisticated. Leisure and business clothing is available in a variety of fabrics that are relatively wrinkle-resistant. Travel accessories and weather gear are available to provide comfort and protection without enormous bulk. And, as I'll show you, there is an effective technique for packing all of these items in a carry-on.

If you want to carry on your luggage, you will need to reorient your packing mentality. Carry-ons are a big change from the 29-inch suitcases you may be used to checking in. The reduced space means that you have to make choices about living on the road. Once you have chosen a traveling lifestyle, you will be able to choose a suitable wardrobe and accessories. This book will *teach* you to travel light.

▼ Carry-on Guidelines

The determination to carry on all their luggage has driven passengers to board with anything and everything imaginable, from computers to giant toys to shopping bags full of pineapples. This might be convenient for the owners, but it wreaks havoc on the other passengers trying to board and on the safety standards promoted by the flight attendants. It is not uncommon for heavy items to rain down from overhead bins during turbulence, injuring passengers and crew. Airline unions have been agitating for stricter regulation and for the airlines to enforce regulations about the number of bags and sizes of carry-on luggage. The Federal Aviation Administration states only that bags that are brought aboard must fit under the seat or in the overhead bin. Each airline is free to define its own limits on the number, size, and weight of carry-on luggage, and it is up to the gate attendants to be as lenient or strict as they care to be.

Their decision is influenced by the size of the aircraft (commuters have less space than jumbo jets do), whether the plane is full, half-full, or empty, and whether it is a long international flight. They may be more lenient toward passengers traveling in first and business class.

Size

Generally, the upper limit for carry-on luggage to be stowed *under the seat* is 45 inches overall. Add up the length, height, and depth of a bag (measured in inches) and the sum should be no more than 45 inches. Bags measuring between 20 and 22 inches long, that is, those measuring 20 inches long, by 16 inches wide, by 9 inches deep; 21 by 13 by 8 inches; or 22 by 14 by 9 inches. The 21-inch and 22-inch models are best for packing wardrobes.

When buying softsided luggage remember that it will expand when packed. Leave yourself some room in expandable bags. For safety reasons and the health of your back muscles, plan to stow your heavier bag under the seat rather than overhead.

Carry-on sizes vary according to the type of airplane you are flying in. Some airlines will allow only 39 inches under the seat, room enough for a small totebag (about 17 inches long). Foreign-based airlines, which also tend to be more strict, commuter airlines, and airlines using smaller aircraft are more likely to have lower limits. Keep in mind that the different aircraft used by the same airline will have different-sized compartments. It is best to call ahead to *each airline you plan to fly on* and ask about its carry-on regulations. Get the information sent or faxed to you, so that you can carry it with you to avoid arbitrary decisions by airline staff. On some aircraft, aisle seats tend to have a bit less luggage space, so, if you have a full-sized underseat bag, ask for a window or middle seat.

The upper limit for baggage to be stowed in an overhead bin is usually 60 inches overall (36 by 14 by 10 inches) but can be as little as 17 by 13 by 9 inches or as much as 20 by 10 by 54 inches. The bin is useful for wider items, such as folded-over garment bags, or longer items, such as duffel bags. For courtesy's sake, try to keep the overhead bin for lighter items.

Number

Most airlines allow you one or two pieces of carry-on luggage. You are also allowed to check through one or two other items, for a *total* of three or four pieces of luggage. So, if you are planning to check additional luggage through, make sure to find out from *each* airline you plan to fly on what your *total* luggage allotment is, with any weight limitations, and how much of it may be carried on.

Counted as carry-on pieces are garment bags, suitcases, briefcases, travelpacks, daypacks, totebags, camera cases, computers and computer cases, shopping bags, and duty-free bags. Remember: You are allowed *up to* a total circumference of 45 inches for underseat luggage, so two small bags that will fit underneath together count as one.

About Garment Bags

Garment bags have their place as carry-on luggage. The general size limitation is 72 inches, or 45 by 23 by 4. They are useful if you are on a business trip or vacation where you'll need suits or formal dresses. If not stuffed too full, they can be brought aboard and stowed in a closet or, folded in half, in the overhead bin. Many people like being able to hang everything up all at once at the hotel.

However, garment bags have great limitations. First, most aircraft have little or no closet space in which to stow these heavy "mobile homes." If you do not get there first, the closet will be full and you will have to stow the bag overhead or check it. Second, meeting the closet's 4-inch-deep limitation will be impossible if the garment bag is packed with the usual requirements for a two- or three-week trip. Folded over, the bag will be too fat to fit overhead so you will have to check it. Among other disadvantages, garment bags are unwieldy to lug if you are taking public transportation on your own, and they do not necessarily prevent wrinkling better than a well-packed suitcase would.

For those reasons, garment bags are not my first choice. Much more useful is a 21-inch or 22-inch carry-on suitcase in the form of a shoulder bag, convertible pack, or wheeled bag.

Additional Carry-on Items

As well as one or two carry-on bags, most airlines allow you to take on board with you other miscellaneous items. These generally, but not always, include a handbag, overcoat or wrap, umbrella, binoculars, camera (35mm, without carrying case), a reasonable quantity of reading material, prosthetic devices (canes, braces, crutches), and unopened liquor, which, if you want to drink, must be served to you by the flight attendants. Travelers with infants are usually allowed an infant-necessities bag, a blanket, a small stroller that can fit overhead, and/or possibly a car seat, if there is room on the plane. Luggage carts may or may not be counted.

Prohibited Items

The following hazardous items, *among others*, are prohibited from being in carry-on or checked luggage: flammables, mace, tear gas and other eye irritants, propane, butane cylinders or refills, cigarette lighter refills, any equipment containing fuel, safety- or "strike-anywhere" matches, solvents, and aerosols. There are certain exceptions for personal care, medical needs, sporting equipment, and items to support physically challenged travelers. For example, flammable toiletry and medicinal articles such as perfume, matches, and lighters may be carried on your person. Pocket knives with blades over 4 inches long are also prohibited unless they are checked. Call your airline regarding any specific item you are concerned about.

Using Portable Electronic Devices on the Plane

Federal regulations prohibit airline passengers from using portable telephones or two-way radios on board. Many other devices can be taken on board but their use is prohibited while the plane is taxiing, taking off, and landing. Each airline has the right to impose its own regulations, and flight crews can impose stricter ones if necessary. Here are some examples. Call your airline to verify pertinent information.

Items generally allowed – Portable voice recorders, electric shavers, calculators, laptop computers with attached mouses, accessory printers and tape drives, handheld electronic games without remote control, typewriters, CD players (sometimes not allowed), electronic toys without remote controls, video camcorders (sometimes not allowed), video players, tape cassette players, beepers, audio tape players, games, pagers.

Items generally not allowed – Radios, AM and FM transmitters and receivers, televisions, portable cellular telephones, electronic games, toys and computers with remote controls, cordless computer mouses, CB radios and other transmitting devices. (From *San Jose Mercury News*, July 4, 1993.)

▼ More Isn't Better— The *Real* Carry-on Allotment

Having just read the list of all the things that the airlines allow you, you overpackers are probably thinking right now, "Great! I can take *everything* with me."

A gentle reminder: Carry-on is not about lugging all your worldly possessions with you wherever you go. Carry-on is about mobility, about freedom, about traveling *light*. The focus of this book is on planning, selecting, and taking *only what you need*.

Our definition of *carry-on* will be *one* manageable carry-on bag that will fit underneath the seat on an airplane and in storage facilities when you are traveling around. For added convenience or a measure of luxury, you may also want to bring a second, smaller bag such as a tote or daypack.

2 | Smart Luggage

Choosing the right luggage is crucial to traveling light. The wrong bag can defeat you if it is too heavy, uncomfortable to carry, cheaply made, the wrong size, the wrong style, or not weatherproof. The right piece of luggage can help you be an organized, self-sufficient traveler, will be a dream to pack, and will be easy to manage. There are three types of luggage suitable for carry-on travel: the 45-inch carry-on (21 or 22 inches in length), the hanging garment bag, and the totebag or daypack. If you are determined to go carry-on and travel freely, limit yourself to the 45-inch bag. Properly packed, it can handle any kind of wardrobe. If mobility is not essential, or you have a larger, bulkier wardrobe, consider the garment bag. Your clothes will not travel wrinkle-free, but these bags provide a convenient hanging closet when you reach your destination.

Garment bags are great for extended business trips as well as for cruises that require a lot of formal wear, but they do have their limitations. They are not reliable carry-ons. Airplane closets fill up quickly. As a result you may have to fold your bag into an overhead compartment. If the bag is packed lightly, it will fit overhead; but if packed fully and folded in half, it could be too large for the overhead compartment and will then have to be checked. Garment bags are also unwieldy to carry about while sightseeing and may be difficult to stow in lockers or on public transportation.

▼ Choosing a 45-Inch Carry-on Bag

Useful 45-inch carry-on styles (21 or 22 inches in length) include the shoulder bag, the travel pack (convertible backpack), and the wheeled bag. To be able to pack as described in this book (see chapter 5), choose a bag with a three-sided zipper that makes it possible to open it flat like a book.

In choosing a bag, consider:

▼ How you want to carry it (on your shoulders, on your back, or by its own wheels)

▼ How much you will be carrying it (take into account types of transportation and activities)

▼ How you want to organize and pack it

▼ Your long-term traveling needs

Shoulder Bags

Shoulder bags are suitcases with a handle and a detachable shoulder strap. Semisoft versions have a structured frame created by piping and foam padding that hold the bag's shape during packing. Their main attraction is ease of organization: they come in one-, two-, and three-compartment designs. If you are carrying a fully loaded shoulder bag, I recommend taking a luggage cart as well. Quality brands include the Easy Going Special Edition Bag, Florentine, Lark, Tumi, Hartmann, Boyt, Andiamo, Samsonite, Land's End, L. L. Bean, REI, Patagonia, and Eagle Creek.

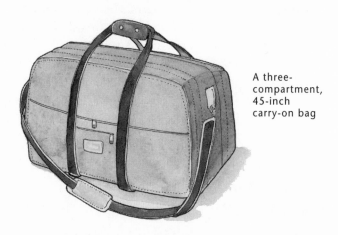

A three-compartment, 45-inch carry-on bag

THREE-COMPARTMENT SHOULDER BAGS

Three-compartment bags are the perfect high-capacity all-purpose bag for extended trips or trips requiring several wardrobes. You can stow warm-weather casual clothing in one section, business or cold-weather wear in the second, and use the third compartment for your accessories. These bags commonly have tie-down straps inside and handy outside pockets for reading materials, file folders, and so on. I use this type of bag myself, and have often shared it with my husband and my kids for weekend trips.

TWO-COMPARTMENT SHOULDER BAGS

Two-section bags are useful for short trips and simple wardrobes. They allow the traveler to separate clothing from accessories or the washed from the unwashed. Additional outside pockets help organize accessories.

A one-compartment bag,
packed with a layer of accessories.

ONE-COMPARTMENT SHOULDER BAGS

People like one-compartment pullman-type bags because they are easy to pack and a single zipper provides access to all their belongings. Some bags come with a movable partition that converts them into a two-compartment bag. Wheels, a selling point for many travelers, are available only on one-compartment bags. Some, such as Florentine's carry-on pullman, come with four wheels and a leash. Others, like the Travelpro Rollaboard, come with two built-in wheels and a telescoping handle.

A travel pack (convertible backpack)
with detachable daypack.

Travel Packs (Convertible Backpacks)

The travel pack, sometimes called a convertible backpack, has become popular because it is versatile and easily carried. These are suitcases that transform themselves. When carried horizontally, they are a single cavity shoulder bag. When turned vertically, the bag can be converted to a backpack: a hip belt and shoulder straps are stowed in the back panel. If you are doing a lot of sightseeing or walking or need to run for connections, it is a real blessing to be able to relieve the shoulders of 80 percent of the weight of your luggage. Many travel packs come with extra features such as side pockets and a detachable daypack (which can act as your second piece of luggage). Keep in mind that, to meet carry-on regulations, such accessories must be emptied or detached for the flight.

Travelers planning to carry on their luggage must choose a convertible pack according to size (the main compartment must be no more than 9 by 14 by 22 inches) rather than fit. Many travel packs come in larger sizes. Unfortunately, they are too large to carry on. Manufacturers of good quality travel packs include Mountain Equipment, Inc. (MEI), Eagle Creek, REI, Patagonia, L. L. Bean, and JanSport.

There are two types of travel packs suitable for general travel:

FRAMELESS TRAVEL PACKS

Frameless travel packs come with padded shoulder straps and an unpadded waistband. You can carry this model on your back or sling one strap over your shoulder for that last dash at the airport. These are suitable for light packers and kids, when loads do not exceed 20 pounds. They are lighter and less expensive than packs with internal frames.

MEI's Silver Streak is a frameless pack that expands when you need it. The main compartment conforms to carry-on size requirements, but by unzipping a hidden compartment you add an extra 4-inch compartment with interior and exterior access.

INTERNAL-FRAME TRAVEL PACKS

Internal-frame travel packs make it easy to carry loads of up to 25 or 30 pounds. Designed to fit your torso, these bags are mounted on two vertical aluminum stays encased in comfortable sleeves. Two padded shoulder straps, a waist-hugging padded hip belt, and a padded lumbar pad balance the weight and eliminate potential muscle strain. Sternum straps allow you to adjust the load.

MEI's Vagabond, with its detachable daypack, can be converted to a light-duty internal-frame backpack. It has pop-out contoured shoulder straps and hip belts and a nonadjustable built-in lumbar pad.

The packs that offer the most body support are the MEI level-I series of internal frame packs. The Flying Scotsman I has fully adjustable shoulder and hip straps, lumbar pad, and parallel stay suspension. The Trekker I is beefier still, and has pockets that can be used to organize the inside or outside of the pack or can be hidden away completely.

Internal-frame packs have three advantages: They are versatile, easily carried, and comfortable. If you want to buy only one bag for year-round use as conventional luggage and for outdoor activities such as hiking or backpacking, buy this style. It will give you the maximum freedom for sightseeing, hiking, and touring around with your luggage in tow. The attached daypack makes it a self-contained unit when you are traveling. Internal frame packs can be fitted to your body, providing the most comfort in a wide range of activities. All packs differ in fit. Buy the one that fits you the best and still meets carry-on regulations. If your torso is long and fit is important for the activities you plan, you may have to choose a larger size and forgo the convenience of carrying it on the aircraft.

Wheeled Bags

Wheeling one's luggage seems to be irresistible. But, before you select wheeled luggage or a luggage cart, assess your needs. If you need one carry-on, a wheeled suitcase or a lightweight luggage cart may be the answer to your prayers. But if you are a constant traveler who carries large loads, if you tend to load the cart with extras, if you have a family, you will need a heavy-duty luggage cart. Extra weight on wheeled suitcases or lightweight carts can cause the handle to bend or even break.

FOUR-WHEELED LUGGAGE WITH LEASH

Many travelers depend on pullmans or rigid bags with four wheels and a leash for towing them. A good example is Florentine's Carry-On Pullman. These bags must be packed evenly so that they do not tip over. They are good for concourses, sidewalks, and parking lots. Detachable or highly durable wheels are essential.

WHEEL-ABOARDS

The hottest new trend in luggage is the one-compartment pullman with a "built-in" luggage cart that has a telescoping handle and two wheels. On all models it is possible to drape a second tote, briefcase, or even a folded garment bag on top of the built-in bag.

These bags, too, are perfect for concourses, airports, and urban travel. (If you will be on rough terrain or in outlying areas, a travel pack or shoulder bag with heavy-duty luggage cart may be more appropriate.) Check the bag carefully. Most of these wheeled models have only a single compartment. Be sure to check the finish, the fabric, and the quality of the wheels and retractable handle before buying. Also, stick to the bag's weight limits. Load it up with extras and you could be in for a broken cart.

The original wheel-aboard carry-on bag is the softsided Rollaboard made by Travelpro. Although the 22-inch model is a one-compartment bag, it has a plastic insert that divides the inner space in half, creating a shelf on which you can place your clothing. A hook allows you to drape a second carry-on over the loaded bag. It also has outside pockets. This model carries up to 100 pounds and costs about $180. Other softsided models include those made by Tumi, Samsonite, Lark, American Tourister, Delsey, Boyt, and Hartmann. On some models the retractable handle reduces the inner dimensions of the bag—don't buy one of these! You need the entire 22-inch space inside for packing.

The "wheel-aboard" bag, with telescoping handle and a hook to hold another bag.

▼ Choosing a Garment Bag

There are numerous garment bags on the market, in all price ranges. Choose the highest quality you can. Consider first the length of your trips, as well as the clothing you will need. Garment bags come in 2- to 4-suit depths, may be 42, 48, 52 or 56 inches long. If you choose a longer version, look for a bag that will fold into thirds so as to fit under the seat or overhead. Some 42-inch models have expandable bottoms.

Choose the lightest possible bag. A simple garment cover will protect that one tuxedo or wear-it-once formal, or suffice for an overnight trip.

A semisoft garment bag is piped to keep its structure. Make sure the outside hook is detachable or stowable so it does not dangle. A bar at the top supports the weight the bag is designed for. Do not over-pack or the bar may bend. Access to the hangers is important, too. Convenient models, such as the Florentine Deluxe Garment Bag, have a self-supporting swing-out curtain. The curtain opens like a door, allowing full access to the interior. A handy hook keeps the curtain out of the way as you pack.

Look for a lightweight, weather- and stain-resistant fabric, such as cordura or ballistic nylon. The hanger system (such as the Wally Lock) should allow use of regular wire hangers and prevent clothes from falling off. Make sure the handle is comfortable. Zipper openings should be oriented correctly whether the bag is in the folded or extended position. Many bags have pockets for accessories, shoes, and soiled clothing; look for an organizational set-up you like. Tie straps inside are handy.

▼ Choosing a Totebag or Daypack

It is nice to have access to items you need on the plane and on day trips without having to return to your main bag. Fanny packs, day-packs, and shoulder totes can hold the day's medicine, glasses, water bottle, a sweater, guidebook, map, writing materials, tissues, lip balm, sunscreen, makeup, a small camera, and so on.

If you do decide to check your luggage through, consider stock-ing your carry-on with an extra shirt, set of underwear, and toiletries so that you will not be entirely inconvenienced if the bag is lost.

Daypacks

The daypack is the most versatile second bag for casual travel. A day-pack can be worn on the back or shoulders, leaving your hands free. You can use it on day hikes, stowing your suitcase in a locker or hotel room. Choose a daypack made of lightweight parachute nylon, pack-cloth, or cordura nylon. Many travel packs conveniently come with a detachable daypack as part of the unit, which is invaluable when boarding and unboarding.

Select a model with at least one pocket on the outside, padded shoulder straps, and a handle at the top. Double zippers allow easy access when the bag is stowed. Attach a combination lock and you have a fairly safe place for your camera.

Shoulder Totes

A lightweight shoulder tote is good for business trips and for touring when you are not doing much walking. It should be big enough to hold a sweater or a change of shoes, in addition to other personal items. Notebook computers and briefcases can be stowed in a totebag, leaving your hands free.

Expandable Bags

I find expandable bags to be indispensable. Made of parachute nylon, they fold up to a size of about 5 inches square and weigh a few ounces. They can easily be tucked into your main bag and used for anything from a totebag to a shopping bag or laundry bag once you reach your destination. You can also use them to bring souvenirs and other extras home. Easy Going sells a wonderful 20-inch carry-on size expandable suitcase with a lockable zipper. Eagle Creek makes a convenient day-pack model.

Fanny Packs

Fanny packs are great for traveling, especially if you do not carry a second bag. For extra security, thread the waistband through your belt loops. Do not use a fanny pack for valuables such as passport, money, tickets, credit cards, and so on. *Those should be carried only in a security wallet.*

▼ General Luggage-Buying Guidelines

Buy the best quality you can afford, and make sure that the manufacturer will service your luggage quickly and inexpensively in case it needs repair. Copy or cut out the luggage checklist at the end of this chapter and take it with you to the store when you shop for luggage.

For all bags, look for the following construction features to determine quality:

SEMISOFT BAGS

Lighter semisoft bags are definitely preferable for the 45-inch carry-on. In most cases they are easier to compress and absorb shock readily. To provide some rigidity, they combine light weight with a structured frame. Sophisticated nylon fabrics in a variety of looks and strengths ward off the dangers of airline mishandling, weather, and general wear and tear.

FABRIC

The fabric should be durable nylon, usually cordura or ballistic, heavy enough to withstand abrasion (at least 1,000-denier or 11-ounce nylon). Ballistic nylon is similar to cordura in strength but is not as resistant to abrasion. Cordura nylon holds up extremely well against abrasion and sharp objects. Vinyl tends to crack or tear over time.

WEATHERPROOFING

Look for polyurethane coating (PUC) of at least 1 or 1¼ ounces on the fabric to prevent moisture from drowning the bag. Other fabrics may have other treatments. Dye should not bleed when wet. Some bags have a Teflon coating for stain resistance.

HANDLE

Look for a comfortable grab handle, either a loop and flap design (two straplike handles joined with a small patch of leather) or single handle (like that on a standard suitcase). Make sure you can easily open and close the retractable handle on a wheeled case and that it will lock into position. I prefer the telescoping handles that are fixed to the widest, rather than to the narrowest, side of the bag. Check all handles to make sure that the hardware and parts are durable.

WHEELS

Wheels should be of rubber or another durable material, and detachable if you intend to check the bag. Make sure the hardware is securely fixed. On roll-aboard bags, look for recessed wheels.

SHOULDER STRAP

The shoulder strap should be wide, adjustable, and removable. Look for good hardware and a nonslip shoulder pad for comfort. Padded replacement shoulder straps are available in specialty travel stores and outdoor equipment stores.

ZIPPERS

Choose double zippers with two pull tabs that come together and close with a little combination or key lock. Double zippers allow easy access even if the bag is stowed beneath the seat in front of you. A plastic coil zipper works smoothly and will not fail if a tooth breaks. Metal zippers have a greater tendency to jam or snag clothing. Large zipper pulls are easier to grasp than small ones are.

STITCHING

Look for double stitching. Finished seams cost more money but will not fray.

FLOOR

The floor distributes the weight of the bag's contents and prevents sagging when the bag is lifted. Bags with structured floors are easier to pack. The floor also determines the way the bag is stored. Most semisoft bags have a padded cardboard or plastic insert to lend structure but allow the bag to be compressed when not in use. Rigid-framed bags have two types of floors: A rigid folding floor means that the floor is attached on only one side. When pressed into place, the bag has a rigid floor; when flipped up, the bag compresses for compact storage. A fixed floor means that the bag cannot be compressed when stored. Soft luggage has no floor reinforcement.

COLOR

Generally, light colors show dirt the most; dark colors tend to show the effects of abrasion fairly quickly.

▼ Luggage Carts

A luggage cart is a collapsible carrier that is ideal for pushing or pulling your luggage along concourses, streets, and even up and down stairs. They are indispensable to many travelers, are generally accepted aboard the aircraft *in addition* to carry-on luggage, and are easily stowed. I strongly recommend a luggage cart if you are taking a shoulder bag.

Carts can accommodate two or more pieces of luggage, making them appropriate for couples or families. You can use a luggage cart with your existing bag if you do not want to buy wheeled luggage. Used with a shoulder bag they make luggage that is effortless to tow, adding immeasurably to your mobility. The best ones are easily collapsed and set up, come with sturdy wheels, a stepslider, and a wide platform for added stability

Assess your long-term needs and your travel lifestyle in choosing a luggage cart. If you travel light, buy a durable, high-quality lightweight cart, such as Remin's FliteLite C525. For long-term multipurpose use, when you are taking heavier loads over various types of surfaces, stairs, and curbs, invest in a heavier duty cart, such as Remin's Concord III, which has large wheels, a wide platform, and stairslides.

Remin Kart-a-Bag makes special models for salespeople who carry computers or sample cases, trade show representatives who carry displays and materials, musicians, photographers, and numerous other mobile business people. The company will lend carts to its customers and offers a one-day turnaround on repairs.

Make sure you buy a durable luggage cart, with unbreakable joints, heavy-duty telescoping tubing, and dependable wheels. It should have:

▼ Adequate carrying capacity—100 pounds is average for the smallest; some will carry up to 175 pounds

▼ The ability to remain upright when put down in a collapsed position

▼ A mechanism to lock it in place when upright so that luggage can be loaded and unloaded easily

▼ High-quality wheels, *at least* 3 inches in diameter (or between 4 and 6 inches for added stability on staircases, curbs, or cobblestones)

- Adequately wide base for multiple bags and added stability
- A size when folded that enables it to fit under the seat or over-head for storage
- A reasonable weight—between 3½ and 7 pounds (naturally the heavier carts are more stable)
- Permanently attached elastic cords on the base

  Optional but highly desirable features include:
- Stair or curb slides
- A garment-bag attachment so that you can drape a dress or suit bag over your luggage

▼ Camera Equipment and Laptop Computers

A camera on a strap is not considered a carry-on. Camera bags or computer bags are, however, considered to be luggage. Therefore you need a multifunction bag. Lightweight, durable camera bags accommodate every camera configuration imaginable. Many models also accommodate laptop and notebook computers. Tenba, Tamrac, Lowepro, Domke, Photoflex, which offers the Galen Rowell line, Sun Dog, Ruff-Pack, and Billingham are well-known manufacturers.

To choose a good bag, pick a case that is comfortable to wear and easy to work from. Many styles exist that are based specifically on your intended activities. There are padded and collapsible shoulder bags (in either full-sized or body-hugging, thin-profile designs), backpacks, bags that double as briefcases or computer bags, fanny packs, and bags that attach to your belt.

If you have a lot of equipment, use two bags. One will transport most of your equipment. A second collapsible model, designed for day use, is easily stored in your main bag when not in use.

Adventure travelers and active photographers prefer fanny packs or modular bags because they allow maximum mobility and leave the hands free. In Photoflex's Galen Rowell line, the main camera bag (either the medium capacity Modular Fanny Pack or the larger Modular Shoulder Bag) can be worn around the waist on a specially designed padded waist belt. Small accessory cases can be added. The waist belt also accommodates the Rowell backpack for clothing. The Photoflex bags have a lid that opens away from you so that you can use both hands for the equipment. Moveable dividers enable you to reconfigure the bag to make room for everything from a long lens to a video recorder.

Lowepro's Orion AW, a fanny pack–style camera bag includes a separate snap-on daypack for clothing, food, and necessities. When not required, the daypack folds neatly into the front pocket of the bag.

Those with a lot of equipment should consider camera backpacks, full-sized bags with adjustable backpack straps and hip belts. Lowepro makes the Photo Trekker in a carry-on size (13 by 6 by 19 inches). Tamrac makes the Super Photo Backpack (12 by 6 by 21 inches) and the smaller Summit Photo BackPack (12 by 6 by 18 inches).

Those who do not need the hip belt will find that many shoulder bags will accommodate equipment and laptop computers. Domke's convenient canvas bag is collapsible. Tamrac bags are also of high quality. Tenba makes bags specifically for laptop computers and the company's Ventures line includes the neat little Airport Express, a nylon mesh see-through film pouch with a handle. It fits into the top of the shoulder bag and is easily detached for hand inspection at the airport X-ray machine. For tips on carrying film, see page 41.

Video tapes, computer disks, and credit cards can all be ruined by the magnetic field found in inspection equipment at the airport. Put these items through the conveyor belt and not the metal detector.

Look for these features when shopping for camera bags:

▼ The outer shell materials should provide protection against impact, abrasion, tearing, and the weather. Ballistic nylon or cordura nylon should be 1,000-denier or more, with a weather-resistant urethane coating. The two fabrics are equally strong but ballistic nylon is less abrasive and looks more elegant than cordura does. Cordura is more abrasion- and slash-resistant. Canvas is not as waterproof or as rugged as synthetics are, but it is lighter, less expensive, less abrasive, and conforms more readily to body shape. Domke and Billingham make fine canvas bags.

▼ Make sure that the inner padding is made of closed-cell foam or other lightweight composite padding, not open-cell foam, which will flatten or degrade over time.

▼ Look for versatile insert walls with movable partitions.

- ▼ Make sure that the buckles and zippers are of high quality, easy to use, and resistant to cold weather.
- ▼ Make sure the pockets have storm flaps for protection in wet weather.
- ▼ A rigid floor prevents the sides from caving in when the bag is lifted.

▼ Luggage Accessories

Here are some items you may need to purchase in addition to your luggage.

Luggage tags – Label your luggage inside and out. For security reasons, use your name and business address and telephone number or your destination address and telephone number.

Retractable luggage lock – This is a cable lock with a combination that allows you to fasten your luggage to a park bench or other stationary object and allows you to take your eyes off the luggage.

Luggage locks – These should be small locks for double-zippered suitcases. I recommend the combination type that you set yourself; there are no keys to lose.

Padded shoulder strap(s)

Pull strap(s)

Luggage straps – These are nylon webbing straps 1, 1½, or 2 inches wide. They offer additional protection in transit.

▼ Luggage Buyer's Checklist: 45-Inch Carry-on Bag

	Model 1	Model 2	Model 3	Model 4
Brand/name				
Store				
Price				
Weight				
Dimensions				
Volume				
Fabric				
Color				
Structured sides				
# compartments	1 2 3	1 2 3	1 2 3	1 2 3
Pockets, outside				
Pockets, inside				
Handle				
Shoulder strap				
Zippers				
Tie straps				
Storage				
Other features				
Travel packs				
Zip-off daypack				
Internal frame				
Frameless				
Other features				
Wheeled bags				
Wheels, recessed or protruding				
Curb skids				
Handle, back or side				
Grab handle, side or top				
Other features				

This checklist is useful in making comparisons among various items of luggage. When considering travel packs and wheeled bags, take the additional elements into consideration as well.

3 | Travel Gear

After choosing luggage, your next priority is putting your travel gear together: equipment and incidentals that you'll need while away from home. Convenience and portability are important, so each item must be chosen carefully. Weight, size, and usefulness are all key considerations. Only pack essentials. If you have room left over, add things that you *might* need. Leave at home items you may only use once or twice. When in doubt, leave it out!

Depending on the type of trip you are taking, where you are going, the length of time you will be gone, etc., you will need different items. Obviously, a business traveler staying in a luxury hotel in New York will not need the same things as an adventure traveler touring rural Asia. Following are checklists, beginning with the bare essentials. You may want to read through all the checklists and descriptions, crossing off items and lists you know you won't need. Then, you can use them when you pack, checking off items as you go.

Note: If you travel often, you can reuse and update the lists, noting items you need and crossing off those things you bring but never use. This will help you cut down on your next trip.

▼ The Bare Essentials Checklist

This list contains items that can become necessary on any trip and provide a minimum level of self-sufficiency—I suggest bringing these along even if you're only going away for the weekend.

- [ ] security wallet
- [ ] travel alarm clock or watch with alarm
- [ ] Packtowl or lightweight towel and washcloth
- [ ] pocket knife (Swiss Army type)
- [ ] toiletries: toothbrush, toothpaste, deodorant, sunscreen, lip balm, razor, nail clipper, moisturizer, shampoo, comb
- [ ] flashlight or reading light

- [ ] bandana or scarf
- [ ] spoon (with a pocketknife and spoon, you can eat almost anything)
- [ ] pen and notebook
- [ ] toilet paper/moist towelettes/Kleenex
- [ ] small camera, film, batteries
- [ ] set of earplugs
- [ ] water bottle and purifier
- [ ] first-aid kit, booklet, medicine
- [ ] all-purpose soap, clothesline, sink stopper, nailbrush
- [ ] plastic bag for wet or soiled items
- [ ] expandable totebag or string bag

Security Wallets

Your first consideration is your method of carrying valuables. I urge you to take some kind of security wallet to carry your passport, money, traveler's checks, credit cards, airline tickets, and an extra copy of your eyeglass and medication prescriptions. *Never put your valuables in a fanny pack, daypack, purse, carry-on, or checked luggage.* These are suitable for a bit of cash for the day, but not for the bulk of your resources. Valuables should go on your person, hidden underneath your clothes. Remember to select clothing that will accommodate the security wallet; assume that you will be wearing it all the time.

In selecting a security wallet consider weather resistance, the type of clothing you will be wearing, and how you want to wear it—around your neck or your waist, under your shoulder, around your leg, or, as a comfortable hanging wallet, tucked along your thigh like a pocket. I prefer adjustable styles such as the World Class Passport Carrier by Coconuts. I do not like neck pouches because the neck straps invite trouble. Even if I have a neck pouch, such as the Undercover Security Wallet made by Eagle Creek, I prefer to wear it around my waist and tucked beneath my skirt, slacks, or shorts. Materials should be weather-resistant. If you are going to tropical climates, choose a cotton- or Cambrelle-backed money pouch—it will be cooler than nylon is—or use one that hangs like a pocket.

WORLD CLASS PASSPORT CARRIER

This is a versatile wallet that can be worn with all styles of clothing. It can be used as a loop wallet, a money belt, or a shoulder holster. The loop has a steel cable running through it. The detachable, adjustable strap also has a steel cable inside so that it cannot be cut off. The nylon pouch has three sections: the front section has a pocket for an American passport and credit cards; the middle zippered section will hold cash and traveler's checks (the money is thus invisible when you need to pull out only your passport at a checkpoint or bank); the rear compartment has room for tickets and other documents. Other nice features include a diagonal zipper, which prevents the contents from falling out, and a polyurethane coating for weather-resistance.

The World Class Passport Carrier, with waistband.

The most comfortable, coolest, and most accessible way to wear a security wallet is to fasten it to your belt or strap it around your waist and then tuck it down your skirt, slacks, or shorts. When you need something in it, pull it up and out, and tuck it back—it remains attached to you at all times.

AROUND-THE-WAIST SECURITY WALLETS

These standard money pouches will hold a passport, money, and tickets. I do not recommend them for hot weather (although when made of cotton they are less uncomfortable), but many people prefer them. Eagle Creek makes a nice line with a Cambrelle-fabric backing that is more absorbent than cotton is and dries much faster.

NECK POUCHES

The best way to wear a neck pouch is actually around your waist, tucked inside your skirt, shorts, or slacks. They are great for unbelted clothing, such as skirts and shorts, and are ideal for women. If you wear it around your neck, do not let the straps show. The Undercover Security Wallet made by Eagle Creek is my favorite because it has an adjustable strap and an outside zip pocket that makes it easy to retrieve a little cash or a credit card without taking the whole thing out.

SHOULDER HOLSTERS

Though access is more difficult, shoulder holsters are generally favored by men. Do not forget to wear them under your shirt, not just under your jacket.

LEG POUCHES

These come in leather or elasticized nylon spandex and fit around the calf or ankle.

MONEY BELTS

These conventional-looking belts have a zippered compartment on the inside for storing folded cash. They come in woven fabric or leather.

WATERTIGHT POUCHES

The Seal Pack, useful for carrying your valuables at the beach, is a convenient, watertight security wallet that can be worn around your waist while you are swimming.

CLOTHING WITH POCKETS

A half-slip with concealed pockets is available from The Primary Layer catalog. For both women and men, Norm Thompson makes Frequent Flyer Jackets with concealed pockets, too. (See Resources for both.)

▼ Money and Travel Documents

These items should be stowed in your security wallet. Pack as applicable:

- ☐ cash/foreign currency
- ☐ credit cards
- ☐ ATM card
- ☐ long-distance calling card
- ☐ traveler's checks (half in your money belt, half in your daybag)
- ☐ airline, bus, and train tickets
- ☐ driver's license or international driver's license
- ☐ list of addresses and emergency phone numbers (including main home contact, a 24-hour travel agent, medical and auto insurance, U.S. embassies and consulates, and doctors at your destination)
- ☐ passport
- ☐ student I.D. card or hostel pass
- ☐ train pass or voucher
- ☐ visa(s)
- ☐ copies of medical and eyeglass or contact lens prescriptions
- ☐ other _____
- ☐ other _____

Other items you may need (these don't go in your security wallet):

- ☐ envelope or resealable plastic bag for collecting receipts
- ☐ wallet or change purse
- ☐ checkbook

Other Documents

In your suitcase store an envelope with photocopies of important documents and any other papers and photographs you might want. Keep the other half of your traveler's checks and half of your prescription medications here, too. Choose yet a third place for your traveler's checks record and list of any PIN and calling-card access codes you need to remember.

For maximum safety, copies of all this information should also be with a home contact person. Keep their phone number in your security wallet. In case of theft, you can call your contact to cancel your cards and send you anything you need.

- ☐ copy of passport
- ☐ copies of medical and eyeglass or contact lens prescriptions
- ☐ vouchers and confirmations
- ☐ other half of your traveler's checks
- ☐ PIN and phone card access codes
- ☐ traveler's checks record
- ☐ medical and auto insurance papers
- ☐ itinerary
- ☐ frequent flyer cards and vouchers
- ☐ sales receipts for any equipment to be declared at customs
- ☐ customs declaration papers
- ☐ immunization certificate
- ☐ health forms
- ☐ list of gifts and sizes
- ☐ other _____
- ☐ other _____

▼ Organizing Your Accessories

Make little kits to be packed in different pouches. For example, assemble all your toiletries in one kit, and make up others for medical needs, laundry, and so on. Small kits allow the most flexibility in using packing space. Color coding makes kits easy to find. Always choose the smallest pouch or organizer that will hold what you need. You can use resealable plastic bags in various sizes (the quart and gallon size are handiest), stuff sacks, colored nylon pouches, or any type of lightweight, slim organizer or toiletry kit. I prefer water-repellent, colorful, zippered nylon pouches, such as those made by Club USA and Outdoor Research. Keeping your kits filled at home speeds up the packing process if you travel often. Personal items can always be packed in the inner spaces of other purses, pockets, or pouches that you plan to take. Make the most of every inch of space.

The following can be helpful when packing and traveling:

▼ **Bags and pouches**

Stuff sacks or nylon pouches are useful both as you pack and on your trip. To pack your wardrobe accessories, I suggest using an 11-by-16-inch pouch to make a "core pouch" for Bundle Method packing (see chapter 5). Plastic bags are good for wet or soiled items.

▼ **Shoe covers**

Use old socks or the fabric bags available in luggage and travel stores to protect clothing and shoes. Do not use plastic bags. Shoes need to breathe.

▼ **Manila envelopes**

Those measuring 9 by 12 inches are useful for sending home brochures, organizing guidebook pages, travel notes, and so on.

▼ **Laundry bag**

Use a pillow case, an Over-the-Door Neat Net, a plastic garbage bag, or an expandable tote.

▼ **2-ounce and 4-ounce plastic bottles**

Transfer any products from large containers into high-quality 2-ounce and 4-ounce plastic squirt bottles. To find out how much you might need, track your consumption before your trip. (Do not forget to take enough contact lens solution—it may be hard to find on the road.) To prevent leaks, leave half an inch of air space at the top of each bottle. Squeeze out the air and close the bottle. You can also tape the tops and store the bottles in a resealable bag. If you don't want to bother, you can buy trial- and travel-sized products at most drug stores.

Other tips:

▼ Choose foil- and plastic-wrapped nail polish remover, shoe polish, facial cleansers, and moist towelettes. Remove all excess packaging.

▼ If you are carrying toilet paper, take only half a roll and remove the inner tube.

- ▼ Transfer general nonprescription drugs and lozenges (such as headache pills, vitamins) into small, clear, rinsed-out plastic film canisters (available at photo developing centers) or small, previously used pill bottles. Label them with masking tape or stick-on labels. Or, you can buy dose containers from drugstores made in a variety of styles by E-Z Dose.

- ▼ Prescription drugs must remain in their original containers. Have the doctor prescribe them in two small bottles. Pack one in your daybag and one in your suitcase.

- ▼ Film canisters can also be used for putting together a sewing kit and for carrying any little odds and ends you need. (Clear ones are more convenient as you can see what's in them immediately.)

▼ Health and Comfort

Following is a checklist for items that will keep you comfortable and healthy as you travel. Think about each one in view of your destination, mode of travel, and personal needs. Rest and sleep are not luxuries but necessities when you are traveling. Consider items like travel pillows carefully, even if they seem like "extras." Your own travel pillow will help you sleep in any hotel room, campground, train, or bus. Look for a durable, washable one. Moon-shaped, inflatable neck pillows with washable twill covers are made by Better Sleep. Down and feather versions can be bought at outdoor stores. Although it takes up a lot of space, the fleece-covered Bucky Pillow is incredible—it feels like a pillow and teddy bear rolled into one. Pillows for the back are also available.

Earplugs are invaluable if you land in a noisy hotel. A good brand is the foam-type E.A.R. If you are extraordinarily sensitive to noise, you might want to consider a Marsona Sound Conditioner. This small electronic device drowns out background noise with the soothing sounds of rain or a waterfall. It comes in single- or dual-voltages, and weighs about a pound. This is unquestionably a luxury, but it might be indispensable to some people.

- ☐ glasses, sunglasses, neckstrap, cases
- ☐ eyeglass repair kit

- [ ] 2 pairs contact lenses
- [ ] contact lens kit or sterilizer
- [ ] eyewash for air travel and/or dusty conditions
- [ ] sunscreen or sunblock
- [ ] lip balm
- [ ] insect repellent (see note below)
- [ ] mosquito headnet or netting
- [ ] water bottle or flask (see note below)
- [ ] water purification tablets or equipment (see note below)
- [ ] ear plugs
- [ ] travel pillow, neck
- [ ] travel pillow, back
- [ ] eyeshades
- [ ] spritz bottle or facial mister
- [ ] prescription medications (carry half in your daybag, half in your main bag)
- [ ] insulated bag for medication, if needed
- [ ] aspirin (or nonaspirin equivalent)
- [ ] antidiarrhea medicine
- [ ] other nonprescription medications (such as decongestants, antacids, throat lozenges, laxatives, etc.)
- [ ] motion sickness medication (see note below)
- [ ] collapsible drinking cup
- [ ] other _____
- [ ] other _____

Insect repellent – N. N-Diethyl metatoluamide, or "Deet," is the main chemical ingredient. Insect repellents, which come in spray, cream, liquid, or solid roll-on, vary in strength from those containing 35 percent Deet to Jungle Juice, which has 95 percent. If you do not want to use a chemical, try natural citronella products. Check with an outdoor or travel store to get the one appropriate for your destination and type of activity. Choose a low dosage for children.

Water bottle or flask – Never underestimate the importance of carrying your own water supply. In hot weather it is essential. The smallest flask should hold at least a quart. A useful type is the collapsible flask: the outside insulating carrier has a velcro belt loop on it so it can be worn on the waist. If you plan to take drink mixes, get a wide-mouth water bottle.

Water purification equipment – Traveler's diarrhea, hepatitis A, cholera, shigella, giardia, and salmonella all can be contracted by drinking the local water supply in many countries. To protect yourself, make sure you have some form of water purification with you. For emergency purposes, carry Potable Aqua: iodine-based, chlorine-free tablets that come in a small bottle an inch and a half high. Add one tablet (two if giardia is suspected) to one quart or liter of water, wait three minutes, shake the bottle, wait ten more minutes before drinking the water (for giardia wait twenty minutes). Designed for emergencies, iodine should not be used on a continuous basis.

For continuous use, the PUR Antimicrobial Water Purifier is recommended. The purifier is a 12-ounce, 5-inch-tall, 2-inch-in-diameter cylindrical pump containing a Tritek cartridge. A microfilter removes all microorganisms (such as giardia cysts) that are larger than one micron, and a tri-iodine resin kills any smaller bacteria and viruses on contact. The result is microbiologically safe drinking water. The replaceable cartridge lasts for 100 gallons, or 1,600 cups of water. It is really convenient to use; you simply remove the clear drinking glass that acts as its cover, open the lid on the plunger, fill the chamber with water, and pump clean water out of a folding spout.

Another compact alternative is the PentaPure Travel Cup. This is a self-contained cup with a purifier (not a filter) unit that fits on top. Simply pour questionable water through the purifier into the cup below, and the water is ready to drink. It processes 100 gallons of drinking water.

Motion sickness medication – This may be medication, an ear-patch, or Sea Bands, which are elasticized wristbands that have a hard plastic bump. When the bands are placed on the wrist, the bump presses an acupressure point that controls balance and nausea. Both wristbands must be worn. People who use these bands swear by them.

First Aid Kit

This kit will handle most minor health problems:

- ☐ emergency first-aid handbook
- ☐ antiseptic pads
- ☐ antibiotic ointment for bites, cuts, sunburn
- ☐ surgical tape
- ☐ gauze bandages
- ☐ Band-aids
- ☐ small scissors (if not on your pocketknife)
- ☐ tweezers or needle (if not on your pocketknife)
- ☐ moleskin or Instant Skin (a medicated aerosol)
- ☐ other _____

Consider these for maximum protection:

- ☐ thermometer (nonmercury type for air travel)
- ☐ Eugenol (oil of cloves)—for toothache
- ☐ Ace bandage
- ☐ cold compress
- ☐ emergency blanket
- ☐ antibiotics, prescription (see note below)
- ☐ other _____

Note: You might want to bring antibiotics if you are going to a very remote area where they may not be available. Check with your doctor.

Toiletries/Personal Items

Choose toiletries carefully and remember that many items will be available at your destination.

I can't say enough about Packtowls. This single item is much more useful than any terrycloth towel. It is a piece of feltlike material called viscose that can hold up to ten times its weight in moisture. Compact and lightweight, it works equally well damp or dry. This quick-drying towel does not fray or pill and is machine- or hand-washable. You can use it as a washcloth or towel; as a dish cloth, sponge, potholder, napkin; as a headband, or dust mask. It is also useful as an emergency compress, bandage, or tourniquet, ankle or splint wrap, marker or flag. I have cut one up into small washcloths and kept them damp in a Ziploc bag to use instead of moist towelettes. If you're traveling with kids, they are invaluable. They come in three sizes: standard, the middle-sized Aquatowl, and the bath-sized Megatowl. Bandanas are also useful, as are large handkerchiefs.

Keep your makeup to a minimum by choosing small sample containers or transferring cosmetics to small jars. When you have only one color combination in your wardrobe, one set of makeup is enough, with lipstick to match your accent or brightest color and eyeshadow, eyeliner, and mascara to match your neutral color. Note: If you will be in a hot climate, take lip pencils. Unlike lipsticks, they do not melt.

Leave personal appliances such as hairdryers home if at all possible, because they are bulky. (For more on electrical appliances, see pages 45–50.) For international travel, take a small dual-voltage dryer with adapters or a single-voltage with a high wattage converter and adapters. Consider an easy-care haircut instead. If you need a curling iron, take one that uses butane, or a dual-voltage iron with adapters for international travel. Note: Butane cartridges cannot be carried on airlines.

It never hurts to carry a small roll of toilet paper (remove the inner core) or a packet of Kleenex with you, and I've been in places where, *thank goodness*, I had seat covers. Foil-wrapped moist towelettes, baby wipes, antibacterial wipes, and so on can be helpful, especially if you are traveling with children. Feminine sanitary products are available worldwide, but U.S. brands are very expensive when purchased abroad. If you don't want to pay extra, take enough tampons or sanitary napkins with you for the entire trip. The O.B. brand is compact. Women can use panty liners in underwear to cut down on laundry.

Women traveling abroad may want to consider bringing a urinary director device. Freshette is a palm-sized, reusable, lightweight plastic device that enables women to stand while urinating with minimal undressing. It is available at REI and other outdoor stores. Le Funelle is the same type of product in disposable form and is stocked by travel specialty shops.

- [ ] Packtowl or lightweight terrycloth towel
- [ ] washcloth (one-third of a Packtowl cut into washcloth sizes, or a thin washcloth)
- [ ] shampoo (or multipurpose soap)
- [ ] conditioner
- [ ] moisturizer (hand, face, body)
- [ ] soap (multipurpose travel soap or bar)
- [ ] shaving supplies
- [ ] deodorant
- [ ] toothbrush/toothpaste/dental floss
- [ ] comb/folding hairbrush
- [ ] toilet paper and seat covers
- [ ] moist towelette packets
- [ ] nail clippers
- [ ] hair dryer
- [ ] other personal appliances (e.g., curling iron)
- [ ] manicure items (nail polish, polish remover)
- [ ] clear nail polish (for runs in nylons)
- [ ] makeup
- [ ] pocket mirror
- [ ] feminine sanitary items (pantiliners, tampons, pads)
- [ ] Freshette or Le Funelle urinary director (for women)
- [ ] contraceptives
- [ ] facial tissue packets
- [ ] bath salts
- [ ] body powder
- [ ] corn or bunion pads
- [ ] removable insoles and other shoe supplies
- [ ] other _____
- [ ] other _____

▼ Room and Security

Do not depend on the hotel's wake-up call. Bring a compact clock that is easy to see at night and easily set. I like bright-colored models (such as red or white) because they are less likely to be forgotten when you are packing hurriedly. For more on security, see chapter 10.

- ☐ travel alarm clock *or* wristwatch with alarm
- ☐ small, good flashlight (with extra batteries and bulb for long trip)
- ☐ nightlight or fluorescent tape for marking light switches
- ☐ portable door lock or rubber doorstop
- ☐ portable "hands-free" reading light with extra batteries and bulb
- ☐ intruder alarm
- ☐ portable smoke alarm
- ☐ extension cord
- ☐ sleep sheet for youth hostels (if needed)
- ☐ mini-safe
- ☐ other _____
- ☐ other _____

▼ Clothing Care

By picking packable fabrics and using the Bundle Method of packing (see chapter 5) and other wrinkle-removal methods (see pages 73–74), you can leave your travel iron or steamer at home. Take one if you want extra insurance against wrinkles. Make sure it is dual voltage for international travel.

A steamer is a plastic vessel with a heating element inside. You fill it with water (in some a bit of salt must be added to speed the steaming), plug it in, and in about five minutes you will have a supply of hot steam that lasts between eight and twelve minutes. Hang up your garment and glide the steamer along to coax the wrinkles out. Steamers are wonderful for removing travel wrinkles in light- and medium-weight fabrics. They weigh much less than irons do, and you can hang the garment up anywhere to steam it. Steamers cannot, however, set a crease in slacks or put the crispness back in a skirt, shirt, or jacket. To do this you need the weight and heat provided by an iron.

Do not expect the same performance from a travel iron as you get from your iron at home. It lacks the weight and heating ability. Still, high-quality models will work well on the road.

A works-in-a-pinch alternative to these electrical appliances is Wrinkle Free, which is a can of deionized water spray that acts as a fabric relaxer on all fabrics except 100-percent polyester and silk. You spray the garment, and use your hand to smooth out the wrinkles.

You can buy or make a tiny sewing kit. Include in a clear plastic film canister needles, straight pins inserted into a small piece of fabric, thread wrapped around a small piece of cardboard, a thimble, several sizes of safety pins, and some basic buttons. You can sew an extra button on the inside of each garment before you go. A small roll of Scotch tape will make an emergency hem.

If you plan to handwash clothes on your trip, you will want to bring some or all of the laundry items in the list below. For tips on cleaning clothes while traveling (and explanations for some of these items), see pages 72–75.

Multipurpose travel soap or detergent is sold in dry packets, solid or liquid in a squeeze bottle. For a clothesline, take the elasticized braided Flexo-line, which does not need clips to hang most items, or 10 feet of nylon cord. Take one or two inflatable hangers for drying blouses and delicates quickly. A sink stopper—the flat, round type—can be helpful; these are often missing from sinks and tubs. For a laundry sack, you can use a plastic bag, a pillowcase, or an Over-the-Door Neat Net bag, which is available at Toys R Us.

If you want to be prepared for stains, take one of these:

▼ A small solid stick or tube of liquid laundry pretreat or stain remover. Products for *washable* fabrics include Cadie, Magic Wand, Shout, Spray'n Wash, or Zout. They must be laundered out.

▼ A spot remover for *dry-cleanable and washable* fabrics. I recommend Goddard's Nonflammable Dry-Cleaning Solvent, an aerosol spray, or a tube of Swiss Care paste.

▼ Spot-remover pads. These will remove stains such as oil, makeup, ink, blood, and food stains from *nonwashable* but colorfast silk and wool fabrics.

- ☐ travel iron or steamer
- ☐ sewing kit
- ☐ multipurpose travel soap
- ☐ clothesline
- ☐ inflatable hanger(s)
- ☐ sink stopper, flat
- ☐ hanger clips or clothespins
- ☐ plastic skirt hangers
- ☐ detergent packets (dry)
- ☐ cold-water soap packets (dry)
- ☐ shoe-shine pads
- ☐ Packtowl
- ☐ lint brush (or use Scotch tape)
- ☐ Wrinkle Free fabric relaxer
- ☐ stain remover
- ☐ detergent, such as Woolite
- ☐ other _____
- ☐ other _____

▼ Entertainment

These are extra things that make travel a little more enjoyable. Take what you have room for. See pages 8 and 45–50 for advice on electronics.

- ☐ books
- ☐ magazines
- ☐ cards, travel games
- ☐ electronic games, recharger, disks
- ☐ portable tape or CD player, headphones and tapes or CDs, tape or CD case
- ☐ travel or shortwave radio
- ☐ microcassette recorder, headphones, and tapes
- ☐ jump rope, inflatable beach ball
- ☐ musical instrument
- ☐ other _____
- ☐ other _____

▼ Sightseeing and Photography

Guidebooks and maps greatly enhance a trip but paper is heavy. To cut down, research thoroughly in advance, photocopy on both sides of the paper those pages you need for your itinerary. You can enlarge or reduce them, cut off the margins, and staple sheets together. Organize them in labeled manila envelopes, for example, Italy, France, and so on. After you use them, give them away to other travelers and fill the empty envelopes with brochures and other memorabilia that you have collected and mail those home periodically.

CARRYING FILM

Label each canister with a stick-on dot and give it a number. In your notebook record the number, then list shots you take. You will know what it is when you get home.

You can buy prepaid Kodalux processing mailers from Kodalux dealers if you want to send film back to the United States as you go. Call Kodalux at (800) 345-6971 for the name of a local dealer.

For film inspection at the airport, place your film in plastic resealable bags and always ask (politely) for hand inspection to avoid the X-ray machine. Kodalux recommends that you do not use commercially available lead-lined bags. They are an invitation to have the X-ray machine turned up. If your camera has film in it always ask for that, too, to be inspected by hand.

- ☐ maps and guides, or reduced photocopied pages from these in labeled 9-by-12-inch manila envelopes
- ☐ magnifier (flat plastic type)
- ☐ compass
- ☐ travel diary, ledger, or small spiral notebooks
- ☐ pens
- ☐ camera, plenty of film, flash
- ☐ filters, lenses
- ☐ dustbag to protect equipment (e.g., pillowcase)
- ☐ extra batteries for camera and flash
- ☐ prepaid film processing mailing envelopes
- ☐ lens cleaner kit
- ☐ video camera, tapes, recharger

- [ ] camera bag, fanny pack, pouch
- [ ] binoculars or opera glasses
- [ ] other _____

▼ Miscellaneous Gear

Eating/Drinking

You may want to bring the following if you will be taking care of some of your own meals and you're unsure what kitchen equipment will be available to you. A Swiss Army knife or similar pocketknife is essential. They come fitted with a variety of tools. Choose the smallest one that has what you really need: a knife, a bottle opener, a can opener, and a corkscrew. Other tools such as tweezers, saw-tooth blades, scissors, and magnifiers are also useful.

The weight of a travel coffee maker makes it worthwhile only for coffee die-hards. If you are going abroad, make sure the coffee maker is a dual-voltage appliance or that you have a converter and the right adapters.

- [ ] flask or water bottle
- [ ] bottle, jar, can opener, corkscrew (if not on your pocketknife)
- [ ] spoon (you can eat almost anything with a spoon and a pocketknife)
- [ ] travel coffee maker
- [ ] utensil set (hot/cold cup, plate, fork, knife, spoon)
- [ ] beverage coil heater (dual-voltage for foreign travel)
- [ ] small cutting board
- [ ] Packtowl or wipe-up cloth
- [ ] bottle stopper
- [ ] all-purpose travel soap
- [ ] insulated cooler bag (foldable)
- [ ] tablecloth or large bandana
- [ ] packets of tea/coffee
- [ ] salt, pepper, spices, condiments
- [ ] liquor (with vodka and an eyedropper you can also disinfect utensils)
- [ ] other _____

Shopping

You can use your regular pocket calculator for currency exchange, but Money Exchange Calculators make handling financial and numerical transactions a breeze. In addition to calculating currency exchanges, they will change centimeters into inches, kilometers into miles, and Celsius into Fahrenheit.

- ☐ string bag, or use your expandable totebag or daypack
- ☐ pocket calculator or currency exchange calculator
- ☐ tape measure
- ☐ magnifying glass (for inspecting jewelry, art, and so on)
- ☐ gift list (with sizes of friends and family members)
- ☐ other _____

Conversation Starters for Foreign Travel

These may be the most important items in your suitcase. They will help you connect with local people.

- ☐ pictures of your home and family
- ☐ language phrasebooks, dictionaries
- ☐ small gifts/postcards from the U.S.
- ☐ other _____

Office Supplies

Remove all packaging and store your supplies in a nylon pouch or Ziploc bag. You may be able to find a small portable office kit that includes many of the items listed here.

- ☐ business cards, calling cards
- ☐ extra stationery or other writing paper, postcards, envelopes
- ☐ Scotch tape
- ☐ Post-its
- ☐ rubber bands
- ☐ paper clips, multiclips
- ☐ small stapler, staples
- ☐ pens
- ☐ permanent marker

☐ mailing supplies if you plan to ship as you go: string, mailing tape, flattened boxes

☐ other _____

Computer Equipment

☐ computer, printer, paper, instructions

☐ modem and foreign phone jack adapters

☐ extra diskettes

☐ battery charger

☐ battery pack(s)

☐ converter, adapter, surge protector

☐ screen cleaning pads

☐ other _____

▼ Dealing with Accumulation

What do you do with all of your guidebook pages, maps, tourist brochures, souvenir admission tickets, and other sundry items you gather along the way? What about purchases? What about film? How do you avoid dragging it all with you?

Paper – Brochures, used maps, guidebooks and photocopied guidebook pages, admission tickets, and so on.

Pack them in 9-by-12-inch manila envelopes labeled with their subject country. When you are done with them, mail them home to yourself.

Souvenirs and cartons – Have the shops ship them home to you or go to a packaging service at your hotel or a post office and ship them home yourself. If you expect to carry a carton home, buy the highly recommended Package Tote, which is a device with a handle and strap. You can affix it to a carton so that you can carry it by the handle. (It is available at some specialty travel and luggage stores.)

Film – Carry film home in clear Ziploc bags or buy prepaid Kodalux developing envelopes from your local dealer before you go. Address them to your home or business.

▼ Electrical Appliances

Traveling with electric appliances can be a nuisance because they are heavy and bulky. Do you really need that hairdryer or iron? If you do, pack the smallest, lightest model (dual-voltage for foreign travel) you can find, with the right adapter plug(s) if you will be out of the country.

Choosing the right electrical configuration for your appliances can be complex. To be able to use the appliance at all, you will need an adapter plug because plugs abroad are all different. To run the appliance you may also need a voltage converter. Consult a travel agent, specialty travel store, luggage store, or merchant specializing in electrical merchandise about the equipment you might need.

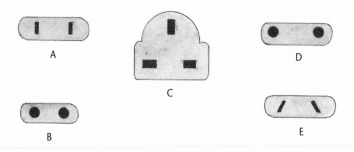

ADAPTER PLUGS

Adapter plugs enable you to use the conventional two-pronged appliance plugs in foreign wall sockets. Worldwide, wall outlets come in five types. In some countries you will find more than one type of wall socket in the same room! Check the illustrations above and the World Guide to Voltages and Outlet Types on pages 46–47, and purchase the right adapter plug(s) for the wall sockets you may encounter. Below are adapters for the most commonly found outlets.

- ▼ Type A - Flat parallel blades
- ▼ Type B - Fat round pins
- ▼ Type C - Three rectangular prongs
- ▼ Type D - Thin round pins (Use this plug for recessed outlets. It acts as an extension on a converter or transformer to accommodate a recessed outlet.)
- ▼ Type E - Flat angled blades

▼ World Guide to Voltages and Outlet Types

Many countries require more than one type of plug. Below are the most commonly found types. For a description of the letter codes, see page 45.

Afghanistan – B/D	Chile – D	Grenada – B/C/D
Aegean Islands – B	China – B/C/D/E	Guadaloupe – D
Algeria* – A/B/C/D	Colombia* – A/D	Guam* – A
Angola – B/D	Congo – D	Guatemala* – A
Antigua – A/B/C	Costa Rica* – A/C	Guinea – D
Argentina – C/D/E	Croatia – D	Guyana* – A/B/C/D
Australia – E	Cuba* – A	Haiti* – A
Austria – D	Cyprus – B/C	Honduras – A
Azores – B/D	Czechoslovakia – B/D	Hong Kong – C
Bahamas* – A	Denmark – D	Hungary – D
Bahrain – B/C	Dominica – B/C	Iceland – B/C/D
Bangladesh – B/D	Dominican Rep.* – A	India – B/D
Barbados* – A	Ecuador* – A/D	Indonesia* – B/D
Belgium – B/D	Egypt – B/C/D	Iran – D
Belize* – A	El Salvador* – A	Iraq – B/C/D
Bermuda* – A/C	England – B/C/D	Ireland – B/D
Bolivia* – A/B/D	Equatorial Guinea – D	Isle of Man – B
Bosnia – D	Estonia – D	Israel – B/D/E
Botswana – B/C	Ethiopia – D	Italy – D
Brazil* – A/D	Faeroe Islands – D	Ivory Coast – B/D
Brunei – B/C	Fiji – E	Jamaica* – A/D
Bulgaria – D	Finland – D	Japan* – A
Burma (Myanmar) – B	France – D	Jordan – B/C/D
Burundi – B/D	French Guiana – B/D	Kampuchea – D
Cameroon* – B/D	Gabon – C/D	Kenya – B/C
Canada* – A/C	Gambia, The – B/C	Korea* – A/D
Canary Islands – D	Germany – B/D	Kuwait – B/C
Cayman Islands* – E	Ghana – B/C/D	Laos – A/D
Central African Rep. – B/D	Gibraltar – B/C/D	Latvia – D
Chad – D	Greece – B/D	Lebanon* – D
Channel Islands – D	Greenland – D	Lesotho – B/D

* 110 volts or a combination of 110 volts and 220 volts; all others 220 volts

Liberia – A/B/C	Norway – D	St. Vincent – B/C
Libya* – B/D	Okinawa* – A	Sudan – B/C/D
Lichtenstein – D	Oman – B/C	Surinam* – D
Lithuania – D	Pakistan – B/D	Swaziland – B/D
Luxembourg – D	Panama* – A/E	Switzerland – B/D
Macao – B/D	Paraguay – D	Syria* – B/D
Madagascar* – D	Peru* – A/D	Tahiti – A
Madeira – B/D	Phillippines* – A/B/D	Taiwan* – A
Majorca – B/D	Poland – D	Tanzania – B/C
Malagasy – D	Portugal – B/D	Thailand – A/D
Malawi – B/C	Puerto Rico* – A	Togo* – D
Malaysia – B/C	Qatar – B/C	Tonga – D/E
Mali – D	Romania – D	Trinidad/Tobago* – A/B/C
Malta – B/C	Russia – A/D	Tunisia* – D
Martinique* – B/D	Rwanda – D	Turkey – D
Mauritania – D	Samoa, Amer.* – A/D/E	Uganda – B/C
Mauritius – B/C/D	Samoa, West – E	United Arab Emir. – B/C
Mexico* – A	Saudi Arabia* – A/B/D	United States* – A
Monaco* – D	Scotland – B/D	Upper Volta – D
Montserrat – A/B/C	Senegal* – D	Uruguay – C/D/E
Morocco* – D	Serbia – D	USSR (former) – D
Mozambique – D/B	Seychelles – B/C	Venezuela* – A
Nepal – B/D	Sierra Leone – B/C/D	Vietnam* – A/D
Neth. Antilles* – A/B/C	Singapore – B/C/D	Virgin Is. (Amer.)* – A
Netherlands – D	South Africa – B/C	Yemen – A/B/C/D
New Caledonia – A/D	Somalia – B/C/D	Yugoslavia (former) – D
New Zealand – E	Spain – A/D	Zaire – D
Nicaragua* – A	Sri Lanka – B/D	Zambia – B/C
Niger – B/D	St. Kitts-Nevis – B/C	Zanzibar – B/C
Nigeria – B/D	St. Lucia – B/C	Zimbabwe – B/C
	St. Maarten* – D	

* 110 volts or a combination of 110 volts and 220 volts; all others 220 volts

Dual-voltage appliances also need adapter plugs. Adapter plugs with grounding pins are more difficult to find but they are available from relocation specialists and some travel stores. They slip onto a three-pronged grounded American plug.

CONVERTERS AND TRANSFORMERS

A converter or transformer allows your 110-volt appliance to run on the 220- or 240-volt current found in foreign countries. (Some countries, such as Japan and Mexico, run on 110 volts, as we do.) If you have dual-voltage appliances, you do not need a converter. All you need to buy is the adapter plugs.

Converters and transformers are designed for intermittent use. Using them continuously may cause the appliances to wear out quickly. Because American appliances are run on 60 cycles and foreign appliances on 50 cycles, your appliance may not work as fast even with a transformer. Hairdryers should be set on low to avoid their overheating. Some models have safety locks that disable the high speed when they are used on 220 or 240 volts.

SINGLE-VOLTAGE APPLIANCES

If you have a single-voltage appliance, read below to determine what kind of converter or transformer you need. There are two types of converters: high-wattage and low-wattage. The one you need depends on how many watts your appliance uses and what type of appliance you have. Note that converters for these two types of appliances are *not* interchangeable.

High-wattage converters (between 50 and 1600 watts) – These are required for heat-producing appliances such as hairdryers, irons, steamers, food or bottle warmers, travel coffee makers, curling irons, and heating coils for beverages.

Low-wattage converters (up to 50 watts) – These are for electronic, *motorized* appliances such as battery rechargers, shavers, contact lens sterilizers, strobes, flashes, massagers, radios, calculators, tape recorders and cassette players, sound conditioners (white noise machines), and video camcorders. Converters for electronic, motorized appliances are also called transformers.

To select a converter:

1. Determine if yours is a heat-producing appliance or a motorized, electronic appliance.
2. Determine the wattage consumption and cycle ratings. They are usually indicated on the item. Always check the actual wattage consumption of the unit to get the proper size of transformer.

OTHER GADGETS YOU MAY NEED

Battery eliminator – This device will let you plug your battery-operated appliance, such as personal tape player, cassette player, or radio (if it has a DC jack), into the wall instead of consuming an endless amount of batteries.

A "reverse" transformer – A device that enables you to use a foreign 220- or 240-volt motorized, electronic appliance (up to 50 watts) on North American 110-volt current. These transformers are useful for visitors to our country and for those things you picked up while traveling.

A heavy-duty transformer – If your equipment's wattage consumption exceeds the ratings of the small converters, you will then need heavy-duty transformers.

Always check the exact consumption to select the right transformer. A good rule of thumb is to double the level. For example, if your appliance is 100 watts, choose a transformer that is 200 watts. Transformers come in 200-, 300-, 500-, 750-, and 1,000-watt sizes and are available in electrical shops or from specialty relocation merchants such as Aris Export (see Resources). Powerful transformers are large and very heavy. Think twice before taking one along.

Motorized, electronic appliances that require large transformers include large radios, stereos, tape decks, large and small food mixers, food processors, blenders, sewing machines, refrigerators, power drills, large medical devices, typewriters, the larger computers, printers, and photocopiers. Many small computers and the laptop and notebook computers come in dual-voltage models. Fax machines do not work reliably even with a transformer. Heat-producing appliances that may require larger transformers include electric blankets, large coffee makers, percolators, and large hot plates.

Some appliances are useless abroad because they only run on 110-volt current; among them are television sets, VCRs, microwave ovens, and clock radios.

4 The Carry-on Wardrobe

If you want to go carry-on instead of hauling lots of bags, you have to choose your wardrobe carefully. Your garments must be packable and, since they are limited, must serve you in a wide variety of social and climatic situations. *Functionality, versatility,* and *style* are your primary considerations. Each may have a different priority depending on the type of trip. The more time you take to refine your wardrobe, the better it will serve you.

▼ How Much to Take

Trips vary in length, climate, activities, and in how mobile and self-sufficient you want to be. Sometimes you want to travel ultra-light, other times you need more clothing choices and don't care as much about the number of bags you have. I have divided wardrobe plans into three approaches and one hybrid. For each trip, pick a packing approach that matches your activities, climate, and mobility and self-sufficiency levels.

The Minimalist Approach

The minimalist travels light. The wash-and-wear wardrobe is perfect for warm weather, for short trips (between three and five days), and for single-purpose trips that are entirely casual or entirely business. You will be washing often and wearing the same outfits frequently. What you need will fit into the smaller 20-inch-long commuter carry-on and the advantage is incredible mobility: you will easily be able to carry all of your luggage on any kind of public transportation.

The Moderate Approach

Most carry-on travelers will take the moderate approach. A basic travel wardrobe of eight or nine pieces will prepare you for temperature swings and varying activities. Your laundry schedule will be somewhat relaxed. You will have several choices for day and evening, an advantage if you will be with the same people continually and would like some variety in your wardrobe. The *moderate* wardrobe is the most that many people can fit comfortably in a carry-on.

The Luxury Approach

For those who prefer to have available as many options in clothing and accessories as possible, the luxury approach is the one to choose. You may be going to formal or business events that require certain types of clothing. You may need to prepare for very cold weather or special activities. The extra convenience may justify a heavier suitcase or even a second bag.

The Multipurpose Approach

Sometimes trips require two distinct wardrobes, both business and casual or for hot and cold weather. If you have the right bag, you can pack two *minimalist* wardrobes and still carry it on. Or you could combine the *minimalist* and *moderate* approaches.

▼ The Basic Moderate Carry-on Wardrobe for Women

For the "moderate" packer (most of us), eight or nine basic garments will create more than twenty different looks. Use this approach for trips of any length (between one week and one year), in varying climates, and for a diversity of activities. This approach will determine the most luggage that you can pack and still carry easily.

The basic eight or nine garments:

- ▼ 1 jacket
- ▼ 1 skirt that coordinates with the jacket
- ▼ 1 pair of slacks that matches or coordinates with the jacket
- ▼ 1 long-sleeved shirt
- ▼ 2 additional shirts or blouses

▼ 1 outfit suitable for both casual and dressy occasions:

a two-piece dress (a blouse and skirt made of the same fabric, which can be a print) with a matching belt or sash, *or*

a skirt or slacks and blouse, *or*

a simple dress

▼ 1 cardigan sweater

Believe it or not, this moderate wardrobe can be worn in at least fifteen different ways.

A SAMPLE PACKING LIST—WOMEN'S MODERATE WARDROBE

Your packing list for a moderate wardrobe, organized by layer, would look like this:

Layer 1—Underlayer

▼ 1 or 2 T-shirts (in cold weather substitute a long-sleeved turtleneck)

▼ 1 extra-large T-shirt for sleepwear or to use as a cover-up in warm weather *or* 1 set of thermal silk or polyester-knit long underwear (for cold weather)

▼ 2–8 sets of underwear

▼ 1 or 2 sets of garment shields

▼ 1 half-slip, if needed

▼ 2 bras

▼ 1 swimsuit

Layer 2—Clothing

▼ 1 three-piece suit *or* 1 coordinating jacket, skirt, and pair of slacks

▼ 1 two-piece dress *or* 1 simple dress *or* 1 blouse and a pair of slacks *or* 1 skirt and a blouse

▼ 1 or 2 blouses, shirts, or blouse-type sweaters; at least 1 long-sleeved

▼ 1 cardigan sweater

▼ 1 pair of walking shorts (optional)

▼ Athletic clothing and underwear, if needed

Layer 3—Outerlayer/Raingear

▼ 1 raincoat *or* windbreaker

Layer 4—The Extremities

▼ 4 pairs of hose

▼ 4 pairs of thin to medium-weight socks

▼ 1 pair of dress shoes (low pumps or dressy flats)

▼ 1 pair of sandals or thongs

▼ 1 pair of walking or athletic shoes

▼ Sun hat; rain hat

▼ Gloves, if needed

Accessories

▼ 1 or 2 belts

▼ 2 or 3 scarves: 1 large square shawl, 1 large square, 1 long rectangular

▼ Simple jewelry (a few basic pieces, but nothing valuable)

▼ 1 umbrella

The Minimalist Wardrobe for Women

The minimalist wardrobe is ideal for short or warm-weather trips. It can be adapted for business or casual wear. If you like, add a pair of walking shorts.

The basic seven garments, which can be mixed and matched however you like:

▼ 1 jacket *or* a cardigan

▼ 1 matching skirt that coordinates with the jacket

▼ 1 pair of slacks that matches or coordinates with the jacket

▼ 1 long-sleeved shirt

▼ 1 outfit suitable for both casual and dressy occasions:

a two-piece dress (a blouse and skirt made of the same fabric, which can be a print) with a matching belt or sash, *or*

a simple dress, *or*

a skirt or a pair of slacks and a blouse

To make up a packing list for the minimalist wardrobe, use that provided above for the moderate wardrobe, substituting your seven basic garments for Layer 2.

The Luxury Wardrobe for Women

The luxury wardrobe will give you the most variety (and the heaviest bag!). It is an expansion of the moderate wardrobe with the addition of two or three items for evening wear, repeated business affairs, or special events. If the fabrics and colors of the extra garments coordinate with all the others and are suitable for day or evening wear (silk, wool crepe, rayon blends), your wardrobe will expand exponentially.

The additional items are:

▼ 1 suit with a blouse (that coordinate with your other clothing), *or*

▼ 1 two-piece dress with a jacket, *or*

▼ 1 blouse, 1 pair of slacks, and a cardigan, *or*

▼ 1 special-event outfit

For the suit, select a solid color or a tweed that coordinates with the original three-piece outfit. Choose an extra blouse in a different style. Keep in mind that you are taking only *one* additional outfit, not all four—you still plan to carry-on your bag!

To make up a packing list, use the one provided for the moderate wardrobe.

▼ The Basic Moderate Carry-on Wardrobe for Men

For the moderate packer (most of us), this is an eight- or nine-piece basic travel wardrobe. Use it for trips of any length between one week and one year, in varying climates, and for a diversity of activities. Men's clothing is large, so this wardrobe may be the most that you can pack in a carry-on bag. Limit the number of garments by selecting versatile styles in compact, packable fabrics.

The basic eight or nine garments:

▼ 1 suit *or* a jacket with coordinating slacks

- ▼ 1 or 2 additional pairs of slacks that coordinate with the jacket
- ▼ 2 short-sleeved shirts
- ▼ 2 long-sleeved shirts
- ▼ 1 dark thin-knit medium-weight sweater

SAMPLE PACKING LIST—MEN'S MODERATE WARDROBE

Here is a sample packing list for a moderate wardrobe, organized by layer:

Layer 1—Underlayer

- ▼ 2 T-shirts (1 extra-large for cover-up or sleepwear, or add pajamas)
- ▼ Silk or polyester thermal underwear (for cold weather; this can double as sleepwear)
- ▼ 2–8 sets undershorts, depending on how frequently you plan to wash them
- ▼ 2–4 undershirts, if desired
- ▼ 1 pair swim trunks

Layer 2—Clothing

- ▼ 1 jacket and 1 pair of slacks *or* 1 suit
- ▼ 2 pairs of slacks for day or evening
- ▼ 4 shirts, at least 2 long-sleeved
- ▼ 1 pullover sweater (V-neck is the most versatile)
- ▼ 1 pair of shorts (optional)
- ▼ Athletic clothing and underwear, if needed

Layer 3—Outerlayer/Raingear

- ▼ Raincoat *or* rainjacket

Layer 4—Extremities

- ▼ 2–7 pairs of dress socks
- ▼ 2–7 pairs of athletic socks (thin and medium weight, drip dry)
- ▼ 1 pair of walking or athletic shoes
- ▼ 1 pair of dress shoes

- ▼ 1 pair of sandals or thongs
- ▼ Sun hat; rain hat
- ▼ Gloves, if needed

Accessories
- ▼ 1 belt
- ▼ 1 or 2 ties
- ▼ Cufflinks and handkerchiefs, if needed
- ▼ Umbrella

The Minimalist Wardrobe for Men

The minimalist travel wardrobe is perfect for short or single-purpose (for example, business or casual) trips. You will be washing fairly often. Vary the sleeve lengths according to climate and style.

The basic six garments:

- ▼ 1 suit *or* 1 sport jacket with 1 pair coordinating slacks in a neutral color *or* 1 medium-weight V-necked or crew-necked sweater with coordinating slacks (you may not need a jacket for a casual trip—a sweater and your rainwear may be sufficient)
- ▼ 1 additional pair of pants that coordinate with the suit or jacket
- ▼ 2 long-sleeved shirts
- ▼ 1 short-sleeved shirt (polo-type knit shirts are versatile)

To make a packing list follow the list above for the moderate wardrobe, substituting your six garments as Layer 2. Add a pair of shorts if you want.

The Luxury Wardrobe for Men

You will need a second bag or a suit bag for the luxury wardrobe. Add to the moderate wardrobe *one* of the following outfits:

- ▼ 1 suit *or*
- ▼ 1 jacket and a pair of slacks *or*
- ▼ 1 sweater and a pair of slacks, *or*
- ▼ 1 special-event outfit

The Multipurpose, Multiclimate
Wardrobe for Women and Men

Assume that your trip requires two distinct wardrobes: one for cold weather, one for warm; or one for business and one for casual. How do you pack for two purposes in a single carry-on? The answer is to pack two minimalist wardrobes (or one minimalist and one moderate), one for each segment of your trip. The three-compartment carry-on is the best bag for such trips. Pack two wardrobes, each in its own compartment, and use the third compartment for toiletries (see chapter 5 for packing instructions).

▼ Clothing Guidelines

Whatever the purpose of the trip, you can assemble a good travel wardrobe by keeping a few guidelines in mind:

- ▼ Take only comfortable clothes, choosing garments that will accommodate a security wallet.
- ▼ Select versatile garments in simple styles.
- ▼ Select compact, easily maintained fabrics.
- ▼ Pack separates.
- ▼ Choose a color scheme and stick to it.
- ▼ Pack clothing that can be layered, rather than bulky garments.
- ▼ Respect local customs.

Meet all these conditions and your clothes will easily go in a carry-on bag!

Such clothes do exist and finding them is a matter of thinking about the requirements and making good choices: simple styles are more likely to be appropriate and not bulky, separates are versatile and comfortable, comfortable clothing is likely to be easily maintained and offer room for a security wallet, and a color scheme and separates will make your wardrobe versatile. That is what this chapter is all about. In it, we will consider the guidelines and consider the various garments that you will be taking.

Comfort

We often give up comfort for fashion's sake. Don't! Choose loose-fitting garments and cushioned, broken-in shoes. Loose-fitting clothes will accommodate under-garment security wallets.

For extended plane, car, and bus travel, wear comfortable, roomy garments that breathe. Loose-fitting skirts or pants with elasticized or drawstring waistbands and shoes that leave room for expanded feet are essential. Take a pair of soft folding slippers, thongs, or thick socks to wear during the flight.

Even if you are a minimalist, you can add a flight outfit to the wardrobe list: a Supplex nylon athletic suit or pair of pants and a T-shirt. You can also wear your principal jacket, skirt, and blouse. Your sweater will remain in your main bag or daybag.

If you are a moderate or luxury traveler, choose any garment combination you plan to take. Wear the heaviest items to reduce your packing load. If you are traveling from a cold climate to a hot one, dress for arrival, not departure. Do not arrive in Hawaii at Christmas in your overcoat!

The Color Scheme

Start with a color scheme. Space is too valuable to be wasted on odd pieces of clothing that cannot be combined with other items. The practical travel wardrobe consists of separates in two colors only. This allows you to mix and match items freely to create different looks. Use a shirt or blouse, scarf, ties, belt, and other accessories to add one or two accent colors. Choosing a color scheme is a central part of creating a travel wardrobe. Limiting yourself to one color combination gives you a framework for shopping. Color can make you feel good, look good, and create appropriate impressions in all kinds of situations. Items that do not fit in the color scheme simply do not go!

Before you try to decide on particular colors, look over your clothes. Do you see a color pattern that you prefer? Do you have enough items of any one color to form the basis for a wardrobe? Research the customs of the countries you plan to visit. In some countries it would be inappropriate for tourists to wear certain colors that have a particular cultural significance. Choose lighter colors for warm weather; medium and darker colors for cooler climates and because they show the dirt less.

Choose neutral tones for the basic pieces of your wardrobe. They are safe and versatile in any situation. Dark and medium colors are also more versatile because they are appropriate for day or evening. Choose solids rather than prints, except for a two-piece dress and perhaps a blouse. They mix and match easily and can be conveniently transformed from day to evening, from casual to fancy. For shirts, blouses, sweaters, and accessories, you can choose from a wider variety of accent colors.

Not all colors are appropriate for all situations and destinations, so consider the shades of the various colors as well.

Neutral, seasonless colors:

▼ Blacks—all shades

▼ Gray—silvery-gray, light and medium gray, charcoal gray, and all in between

▼ Neutral beiges—beige, camel, taupe, tan, khaki, cream, ivory, sand

▼ Brown—cocoa, rust, chocolate, smoke brown, and others

▼ Navy—nautical, bright, black navy, royal

If you like to wear a little more color, consider:

▼ Bright neutrals—red, teal, purple, jade

▼ Deep neutrals—forest green, hunter green, deep teal, burgundy, rust, copper, plum, cocoa, tan, taupe, khaki

These colors can be used as accents, too. The following neutrals only work in spring and summer but may be worn as accents all year long:

▼ Pastels, light and dark—pink, yellow, mint green, lavender, peach

▼ White—seasonless in shirts and blouses only; in other pieces, such as jackets, dresses, slacks, and so on, it is for summer only.

The charts on page 61 show color combinations derived from neutral schemes. Once the basic wardrobe pieces and shoes have been chosen, add other blouses, shirts, shoes, and accessories in coordinating accent colors.

▼ Wardrobe Color Planner—Women

First neutral color (for jackets, skirts, and slacks)	beige	navy	black	bright	gray
Second neutral color (for shirts, blouses, and sweaters)	navy white or ivory black *casual only:* pastels bright neutrals deep neutrals	neutral beiges white or ivory burgundy gray *casual only:* deep neutrals bright neutrals	white or ivory khaki taupe gray bright neutrals	black white or ivory gray navy neutral beiges	white or ivory black camel navy *casual only:* pink peach yellow
Shoes, belts, and handbags	neutral brown	navy	black gray	black	gray black neutral
Accent colors (for accessories, blouses, jewelry)	earth tones gold ivory bright colors deep colors	red burgundy gold silver bright colors	red gold white ivory silver	silver gold brights white ivory	red burgundy deep green pastels silver gold

▼ Wardrobe Color Planner—Men

First neutral color (for suits, jackets, and slacks)	beige/brown	navy	black	gray
Second neutral color (for shirt and second pair of slacks)	white or ivory brown any other beige	neutral beige white or ivory burgundy gray	gray white or ivory	black navy burgundy
Shoes and belts	brown	black	black	black
Accent colors	earth tones burgundy or red pastels brights deeps	gold red hunter green	red	burgundy red

▼ Recommended Fabrics for Travel Wardrobes

	Cold to mild climates (3-season)	Warm to hot climates
Jackets, skirts, slacks, and shorts *Choose medium- to light-weight fabrics for year-round wearability. Wool gabardine and knits are especially recommended.*	100% wool gabardine wool/synthetic blends 100% polyester (i.e., microfiber) wool jersey knits synthetic suede rayon and rayon blends cotton jersey knits, heavier weight viscose blends	lightweight wool gabardine cotton or cotton/polyester knits natural/synthetic blends with linen look viscose and other synthetic blends 100% cotton* cotton/polyester polyester crepe de chine handwashable silk* silk—raw, hopsack, and tweed* supplex nylon
Sweaters/ warm shirts *Choose thin and medium weights.*	100% wool (angora, cashmere, lambswool, merino, and so on) wool and synthetic blends 100% acrylic cotton/cotton blend knits in heavier weights Polartec fleece wool flannel	100% cotton knits cotton/polyester knits cotton/silk blends cotton/linen blends* cotton chamois or flannel
Shirts/blouses	cotton/synthetic blends polyester crepe de chine rayon and rayon crepe* various synthetic blends silk jacquard and other silks* silklike synthetics	cotton knits cotton/viscose cotton/synthetic blends polyester crepe de chine various natural/synthetic blends 100% cotton*
Dresses and 2-piece dresses	wool jersey knits wool and synthetic blend knits wool or rayon challis* washable silk and raw silk* cotton knits, heavy weight various synthetic blends (including viscose acetate, etc.)	cotton and cotton blend knits cotton crepe or gauze cotton/polyester blends rayon crepe* linen/synthetic blends various natural/synthetic blends

* Needs ironing or steaming

Separates

Separates allow you to mix and match easily and extend the uses of your wardrobe. They are also easier to pack. A two-piece dress, a skirt and blouse made of the same fabric in a solid, stripe, or print, can be your most versatile garment. In a knit, washable silk, or rayon crepe it can be worn for day or evening, for casual or dressy occasions. It can also be mixed and matched with your other items in many combinations. (Dresses are bulkier to pack and limit access to your security wallet. If you must take one, choose a very simple, neutral color chemise or shirtwaist dress in a fabric that can be worn in the day or evening.)

Other excellent choices are the unstructured jacket or blazer with ample room for layering; A-line, straight, wrap-around, or not-too-full skirts (with pockets); split skirts; shirts and blouses in scoop-neck, campshirt, turtleneck, button-down, and polo styles; and coordinated knit sweater or jacket sets. All your garments should have pockets.

Multifunctional Garments

Stay away from jumpsuits and dresses that are designed for specific functions. Look at every garment and think of the different ways you can wear it: a large T-shirt can replace a robe, beach cover-up, and sleepwear. Long underwear or cotton tights or leggings can be worn in bed. A skirt and blouse in the same fabric can be a two-piece dress or two separate outfits. A simple button-down campshirt can be casual or dressy. Polo shirts are more versatile than conventional T-shirts and protect one's neck from the sun as well. Walking shorts can double as swim trunks. A sweater with gold buttons can be casual or dressy. If it has a V-neck and no pockets it can also be worn backwards.

Simple Styles

Simplicity will get you by in any situation, casual or dressy. You can also get years of wear out of your wardrobe if you choose classic styles. Simple styles are also easier to pack; drapey skirts and pleats are more difficult and more time consuming to care for on the road. Also, a classic look guarantees acceptance in most parts of the world, no matter what the custom.

Sleepwear and Loungewear

Nothing feels as comforting after a long day of sightseeing as curling up in your hotel room with a good book. But loungewear and sleepwear consume lots of space. When choosing specific items, keep these tips in mind.

A dress-length T-shirt can be worn as a nightgown and as a swim cover-up, bathrobe, or even a dress (add a nice belt or sash). For insulation, wear long underwear underneath or a turtleneck.

For leg warmth, add silk-, cotton-, or polyester-knit leggings.

Athletic leggings can also be worn for exercise.

Sleep in long underwear. Silk- or polyester-knit shirts and leggings will keep you warm and are cozy to wear. Try a medium weight.

If you still want conventional sleepwear, choose, instead of a nightgown and robe, a packable pajama set that looks nice enough to wear down the hall. The Primary Layer catalog (see Resources) for more on pajamas.

Robes take up too much space in a carry-on. Plan on wearing your pajamas, raincoat, or long T-shirt instead.

Maintenance

Choose the type and amount of clothing that you will be able to maintain according to the laundry services available. Are you going to do your own wash? How often? Are there dry cleaners where you are going? Are there laundromats? Take great care in choosing fabrics. Decide whether you want to lug an iron or steamer. If you do not, stick to wrinkle-resistant, drip-dry, hand washables. Find out about the cost, quality, and availability of dry cleaning before taking lots of dry-clean-only fabrics. Make sure you know how to remove stains (see pages 74–75) and carry stain-removing supplies with you (see page 39).

I suggest taking two pairs of removable garment shields. These are perspiration guards that you slip over your bra under your shirt or dress. They will cut your laundry load in half, because you do not have to wash merely because of perspiration. They are available in fabric stores.

Formal Wear or Special Events

Even cruises that have one or two formal evenings no longer require evening gowns and tuxedoes; in most cases a silky dress and a coat and tie are the norm. For formal events and evening wear select elegant packable fabrics such as a silky synthetic, wool knit, rayon crepe, and synthetic blends. Use accessories to add flair.

No matter what packing approach you have chosen, dress-up wear will be limited. For the minimalist traveler, the two-piece dress, a skirt or slacks and dressy blouse or cardigan with a bright scarf or belt might be as dressy as you get. Moderate and luxury travelers have a bit more choice in the two-piece dress and another dressier outfit. But all is not hopeless. A V-neck cardigan can be worn backwards for a deep V-back, with pearls. A simple chemise dress can be dressed up with a scarf and necklace. Pants and blouse or a two-piece dress in a silky fabric will be very lightweight and compact. A black rayon crepe split skirt and blouse or a pastel chiffon-type skirt and a blouse make compact evening wear.

Respecting Local Customs

Research the areas you are going to visit. Consult your travel agent, guidebooks, and experienced travelers to find out about the standards of acceptable dress. In many foreign countries modesty is the norm. Clothing should not be revealing in any way. Women should bring a scarf to cover the head and shoulders at religious sites. Avoid wearing shorts and low-cut blouses, skirts above the knee, and swimwear when you are away from the beach. If you must bring shorts choose a baggy, knee-length style.

The climate of your destination can dictate your choice of color. Sunny places and informal cultures call for light, bright colors. In the large, older metropolitan cities in Europe and South America, tailored clothes in neutral and dark colors are more the norm. The color black is accepted as modern and sophisticated all year long in many large metropolitan cities in Europe, South America, and the United States. It may, however, look too somber in sunny Asian cities, the Mediterranean, and other coastal resort areas.

Clothing styles vary from city to city, even in the United States. Some countries require more formal dress; others are less restrictive. For example, in European cities slacks are generally not worn by women to work or in dressy restaurants. Suit jackets are worn in offices, restaurants, and on the street. In India, a conservative suit would be inappropriate among the bright colored saris.

The safest strategy is to be tastefully dressed, perhaps on the conservative side. This means a jacket and tie (or a dark sweater and tie) for men, and a skirt and blouse or shirtwaist dress for women. For casual occasions, a button-down or polo-style shirt with short or long sleeves will always look appropriate. You can buy garments of the local style in the country you are visiting. Casual clothes such as jeans, jogging suits, athletic shoes, T-shirts, shorts, and resort wear will mark you as a tourist and should be reserved for the outdoors and resort areas.

In the Middle East and Asia, shoes are often removed in homes and temples and mosques. Take shoes that are easy to put on and take off. (For visiting temples, tennis socks can be tucked in your daybag.) Observe your host and those around you to determine whether shoes are appropriate.

Bikinis are not acceptable at many destinations, and worn only by tourists in others. In resort areas that attract an international clientele they are the norm. Ask your travel agent for advice and travel with a conservative one-piece suit unless you are sure a bikini is permissible.

Layering—Adjusting for Climate

The best approach is to pack thin layers of clothing that can be added or peeled off as the temperature changes. Avoid packing bulky sweaters and coats unless they are absolutely necessary. (If you need heavy items for only part of your trip, consider sending them home after you are finished using them.) The concept of layering is so important that I have organized all my travel wardrobes around it.

Layering means wearing several complementary lightweight garments rather than one or two bulky ones. Because different fabrics and fibers have different qualities, the layering pieces must be made in appropriate fibers, weights, and fabrics so that warmth, ventilation, and wind- and moisture-resistance will be provided without hindering your mobility.

There are four basic elements to the layering system: an under-layer, an insulating layer, an outer layer, and clothing for the extremities.

LAYER 1—THE UNDERLAYER

The first layer is worn against the skin and has two functions. The first is to allow excess body heat to be released; for this, use a fabric that can breathe such as a knit or other open weave. The second is to carry (wick) perspiration away from the body. In warm weather, moisture should be absorbed by the fabric, keeping the body dry. In cold weather, moisture should be transferred (wicked) away from the skin to the outer layers of the clothing, where it evaporates. Thus the body is kept warm and dry, even in wet weather.

Warm-weather underlayers – Cotton knit is great for the under-layer, even when it is your only layer. The material is comfortable, absorbs perspiration, and has a quick-cooling effect. Being compact, it also fits easily into your bag. T-shirts are the perfect foundation for a layering system. Choose a variety of styles to be dressed up or down. Polo-type shirts are especially versatile and protect your neck from the sun as well.

Cotton-blend leggings and tights are excellent leg insulators. A pair of these with a big T-shirt will give you pajamas and lounge-wear, too.

Underpants should be of cotton or mostly cotton with some polyester. So that they will dry faster, choose a lightweight open weave, in the smallest style you can wear. For ventilation, men should pack woven boxer shorts.

Cold-weather underlayers – Used widely for outdoor clothing, modified polyester knits wick moisture away to the outer layers faster than natural fibers will. Polyester readily repels water, remains rela-tively warm when wet, and dries quickly. The new treated polyester knits, such as Capilene (made by Patagonia), Moisture Transfer System (MTS, made by REI), polypropylene, and Thermax all have insulating properties. Capilene, MTS, and Thermax are machine washable and dryable, and do not retain odors. Undershirts, pants, shorts, hats, socks, and gloves are all made from the comfortable materials.

Silk long underwear also provides lightweight, bulkless warmth. It is most suitable as a comfortable layer beneath street clothes. It is also great as sleepwear. The strong silk fibers retain body heat and the fabric can breathe. Available for men and women in all styles of shirts, camisoles, long underwear, briefs, and turtlenecks, silk underwear is hand washable and drip-dries quickly.

Silk underwear is available throughout the year from the mail-order companies Wintersilks and the Primary Layer. Seasonally it is available from Eddie Bauer and Norm Thompson catalogs. Polyester-knit underwear is available year-round from mail order catalogs such as REI and Patagonia, and in outdoor stores. Seasonally it is also available from L. L. Bean and Land's End.

Use lightweight fabrics for highly aerobic activity, medium for stop-and-go and general travel, and heavy for extremely cold climates. If in doubt, it is best to err on the side of lightness; you can always adjust the outer layers for added warmth. Bring extra underwear for cold-weather destinations as it will dry slowly. Nylon and silk dry faster than cotton. Note: Both silk and cotton lose their insulating abilities when wet.

LAYER 2—INSULATING LAYERS (REGULAR CLOTHING)

The insulating layers, in the form of shirts, slacks, and sweaters and jackets are an integral part of the system. They trap air and keep the body warm, offer protection from sunburn, mosquitoes, and so on, and should also wick moisture toward the outside. The particular garments you choose will depend on the weather.

Warm and hot climates – Shirts will be worn alone to ventilate the body, or layered over your T-shirt (which is Layer 1) to keep the chill off or protect you from the mosquitoes and the sun. For maximum versatility take loose-fitting, lightweight, button-down shirts and blouses made from cotton or cotton and polyester woven or knit fabrics. For wet or humid conditions open-weave cotton or cotton mixed with Supplex nylon feels natural, is wrinkle-resistant, and dries quickly. Patagonia, TravelSmith, Norm Thompson, and L. L. Bean sell clothing that is ideal for casual or dressy situations in warm and tropical weather.

For men's dress shirts, the coarser weaves such as oxford cloth do better when packed in a carry-on. Silk is packable, but make sure it is hand washable and take along a stain remover for silk—it is very delicate and hard to treat when stained. Finely woven cottons wrinkle very easily—forget them. For casual sightseeing trips, pack shirts of cotton and cotton/ polyester blends. I recommend a wrinkle-resistant weave, such as chambray, twill, or seersucker, or a garment-washed fabric in a light to medium weight. Do not expect the pressed look unless you plan to bring an iron. Make sure to take a lightweight long-sleeved shirt (and hat) for sun protection.

For warm weather a thin cotton or cotton blend knit cardigan or pullover sweater is perfect. For women cardigans are definitely the most versatile: They go with shorts, skirts, and slacks. If the cardigan has no pockets and a V-neck, you may also be able to wear it backwards for two different looks. If you expect temperatures to drop, take a cotton flannel or chamois-type shirt, a thin wool sweater, or a lightweight polarfleece jacket or vest. Polarfleece is just as warm as wool but is lighter, more compact, and dries quickly. It is available under various brand names from L. L. Bean, REI, Patagonia, and other outdoor catalogs and retailers.

Jackets such as sport coats and blazers must be made of breathable, pliable, wrinkle-resistant fabric. Tropical- or medium-weight worsted or gabardine wool or wool blends, cotton and polyester blends, polyester microfiber, some silks, cotton, and linen-look blends are all recommended. Spandex is added to many fabrics now to improve their flexibility and comfort. Wrinkle-resistant travel jackets available by mail order from Norm Thompson include an eleven-pocket Frequent Flyer Jacket (65 percent polyester and 35 percent wool) and a seven-pocket Stretch Twill Travel Jacket (cotton and polyester). The Frequent Flyer comes in a four-pocket version for women. Patagonia offers a 100 percent microfiber jacket. TravelSmith, L. L. Bean, and Land's End also offer excellent sport coats for travel. These jackets typically come in khaki, navy, olive, and brown. Darker colors such as navy will give you maximum versatility for casual and dress wear.

The world is increasingly informal and you can get by in many places around the world without a sport coat. A dark pullover sweater, nice slacks, white shirt, and tie will do just fine. Jackets are, however, appropriate in cities for good restaurants and on cruises for the formal nights. Jackets are essential if you are doing any kind of business. In many parts of the world they are necessary unless you are on a casual trip. Ask your travel agent or host for advice. If you do take one, try "the uniform"—navy blazer, gray and/or tan slacks, white shirt, burgundy sweater, tie. This look is appropriate for any occasion.

Women can base their entire wardrobe around the versatile two-piece dress. In a fabric that is suitable for day or evening such as knit or a rayon crepe, the matching skirt and top will give you lots of clothing options. Worn as a dress, the outfit can be formal enough for theater or dinner; worn separately the pieces can be mixed and matched with the other pieces. If the top is in a button-down style with a straight finished bottom, it can be tucked in or worn out or layered over other tops as a light jacket. A two-piece dress is far easier to pack than a one-piece dress is.

If you must take a dress, look for a neutral, chemise-style dress in a cotton or wool knit that can be transformed easily for day and evening. For warm weather a cotton shirtwaist dress is useful. Remember that dresses are bulkier to pack than skirts and blouses are.

Slacks, skirts, and shorts should be made of cotton, cotton and polyester, or lightweight wool. Twill is a sturdy and versatile weave. Spandex makes clothing comfortable even on long plane rides. Roomy pants and shorts are available in Supplex nylon which is compact, light, and cool. An extremely wind-resistant fabric, it dries quickly in hot weather, making it ideal for beach, desert, boat, and other warm weather vacations. Being compact, it also makes a good choice for athletic suits.

Slacks should be loose fitting for ventilation and should not chafe. Jeans do not travel well unless you have access to a washer and dryer; they are heavy, cold, and dry slowly when wet.

Skirts should have pockets, be mid-length, and simply styled. They should also be loose fitting and allow the use of a security wallet. I also like skorts or culottes.

Shorts should be knee-length with lots of pockets. Supplex nylon shorts will double for swim trunks and casual wear; look for the longer versions.

Temperate to cold weather – In cool to cold weather, choose jackets, slacks, and skirts in light- and medium-weight wool and wool blends or heavier cotton and cotton blends. Polyester microfiber is also light but warm. Wool knits are excellent for dresses and women's coordinates. Sweaters and cardigans should be made of thin wool or wool-blend knits. For blouses, year-round silks and synthetics are fine. Add layering pieces such as turtlenecks and long-sleeved shirts of cotton knit, chamois, or wool flannel. Fleece jackets or vests provide excellent insulation.

LAYER 3—OUTERWEAR/RAINGEAR

The top layer protects you from wind and moisture while allowing body heat to escape. Often a simple shell over your previous layers is all you need to do the job. In outerwear there is no perfect fabric that does everything—some breathe, others are waterproof. Choose according to your needs. For hiking you need a waterproof fabric; for skiing you need a fabric that breathes; for sightseeing, you need style and water repellency. Pick a packable version. Keep in mind that if you are packing light, a heavy coat will have to be worn or carried on your arm.

LAYER 4—THE EXTREMITIES

Bring a hat that is appropriate for rain or sun. Balaclavas, headguards, and headbands for ear covering, should all be considered for cold weather. Polyester (for example, Capilene) or silk knit gloves weigh little.

Socks should be in thin and medium weights that can be layered and will dry quickly. Cotton with nylon or other synthetics will wick moisture away from the foot. For hot weather, socks with a high percentage of cotton will be the most comfortable. They are not good for cold or wet weather, as cotton loses its insulating ability when wet. Wool socks may be necessary for hiking. Many blends are available at outdoor stores. I like silk or polyester knit sock liners. You can wear them under thin fast-drying socks for added insulation. Tights instead of hose keep you warm in cold weather.

You may also want to invest in a lightweight packable pair of galoshes to cover your shoes for rain or spray Scotchguard on your shoes to protect them.

▼ Clothing Care on the Road

Plan on doing a little laundry every night or every other night instead of saving it all up. This way you'll need to take fewer clothes.

Check all garment labels for specific care requirements. Be sure to choose fabrics that are easily washed on the road. Always use a gentle soap and not harsh detergents for washing. Clothes-washing items you might want to bring are listed on pages 38–40.

HANDWASHING COTTON, SILK, AND DELICATES

1. Fill the sink or tub with lukewarm water. Add a *mild* liquid detergent or a cold-water detergent such as Woolite.
2. Swish the garment (do not squeeze, twist, or rub it) for a couple of minutes.
3. Rinse thoroughly in cold water.
4. Lay the wet garment on a towel (a Packtowl is ideal for this) and roll it up to remove excess water.
5. Hang cottons, synthetics, and natural and synthetic blends to dry. Iron cottons with moderate to high heat, synthetics and blends with low heat.

Woven silk should be ironed, dry or with steam, *while still wet*, until the garment is dry. Use a press cloth. To avoid wrinkles wash only what you have time to press immediately. It is hard to get wrinkles out after clothes have dried.

HANDWASHING WOOL AND OTHER SWEATERS

Caution: Wool takes time to dry except in very hot, dry weather.

1. Fill the sink with cool or cold water. Add a cold-water detergent such as Woolite.
2. Soak garment for three minutes.
3. Squeeze soapy water very gently through the sweater.
4. Rinse thoroughly in cool or cold water.

5. Roll the sweater in a Packtowl or ordinary towel to remove excess moisture. Do not wring or twist.

6. Dry the sweater flat. Block it to the original size if needed.

REMOVING WRINKLES

Hang out tomorrow's outfit to get the closet wrinkles out. Remember to take an extension cord and adapter plugs to use with your iron (and a converter if it is not dual voltage). Be sure the garments are cool and dry before wearing them. If they are still warm, the pressing will fall out.

Ironing – Use an iron to add crispness to a garment (such as those of cotton or linen) and to press creases *in*.

1. Turn down the bedcovers to create an ironing surface.

2. Test the iron heat on the underside, hidden edge of the fabric first. Synthetics take low heat; natural fibers take higher heat.

3. Press garments on the wrong side with a press cloth to prevent shine or scorch. (A large handkerchief or a used sheet of fabric-softener works as a press cloth and allows you to see what you are doing.)

4. If desired, use spray starch to keep cotton looking crisp.

5. Do not move or wear garment until it is completely cool.

Steam-and-dry – This method makes wrinkles fall out of dry clothes.

1. Hang one or a few sets of clothes in the bathroom.

2. Turn on the hot water in the shower or bathtub.

3. Wet your hand and glide it vertically down the garment, moistening the fabric.

4. When the shower is steaming or the tub is between one-third and half full, turn off the water.

5. Leave the clothes hanging up for thirty minutes or up to two hours, depending on the fabric. Wools, wool blends, and most synthetic blends steam out well, as do most linen and cotton blends. Silks and cottons should not be left to steam, because they are so absorbent.

6. Let clothes air dry before wearing them.

Travel steamer – Use a steamer to remove travel wrinkles and creases. Steamers are lighter than irons and may be used anywhere in the room where you can hang a garment—you need not create an ironing surface. They work best on light and medium fabric but cannot be used to crisp and press a garment.

1. Hang up garment from a door or window rod.
2. Fill the steamer as indicated, wait about five minutes for steam to develop. (You can add a pinch of salt to hasten the process.)
3. Glide the steaming head along the garment, pulling and smoothing the fabric with the other hand as you go. Wrinkles should fall out easily.
4. Make sure that you empty, rinse, and dry the steamer after each use, according to instructions.

Quick method – Wrinkle-Free is a commercial fabric-relaxer spray to be found in drugstores, travel stores, and luggage shops. It can remove wrinkles from almost all fabrics, except for 100 percent polyester. It is a spot treatment and works best on absorbent fabrics such as cotton, wool, and silk. To use, spray the garment, smoothing out the wrinkles by hand.

STAIN REMOVAL

Part of maintaining your clothes on the road is dealing with the inevitable stains acquired while picnicking, in restaurants, and in general activity. The best guide on the subject is Don Aslett's *Stainbuster's Bible: The Complete Guide to Spot Removal* (Plume, 1990). If you prefer to use natural ingredients, read *Clean & Green: The Complete Guide to Nontoxic and Environmentally Safe Housekeeping* by Annie Berthold-Bond (Ceres Press, 1990).

Before you start trying to remove a stain, make sure you know what kind of fabric you are working with and what caused the stain. Check the clothing tag; some stain-removal agents should not be used on certain fabrics. General procedures:

▼ Treat stains *immediately, before they set.* Sponge or rinse with cool water or club soda. Fresh stains are much easier to remove.

▼ Do *not* apply heat from hot water, an iron, or a dryer until stain is removed. Heat will set most stains. Start with cold water, then go on to warm.

▼ Test the garment for colorfastness by using the agent first on a hidden inside seam or the hem. Bleach and ammonia should be diluted before being used at all.

▼ First blot, absorb, or scrape off all excess liquid or solids, thus removing much of the potential stain.

▼ Remove stains by blotting, flushing (applying liquid so it flows through the fabric), or rinsing, not by rubbing.

▼ Apply stain removers and rinsing liquid to the back of the stain. When applying always work from the *outside in* to contain the stain.

▼ Rinsing a dry-cleanable item means to sponge-rinse with a wet clean cloth. Put a dry cloth on the opposite side to absorb excess water as you rinse. Never flush a dry-cleanable garment.

▼ Avoid leaving a ring by "feathering" or blending the edges of the wet spot into the dry area after each rinse. Lightly wipe off with a lifting motion from the inside out.

▼ Take dry cleanables in immediately for professional treatment if possible.

▼ Shoes

The quest for comfortable travel shoes should equal your determination to travel light. Comfort has to be the top priority when you are purchasing shoes. Luckily several manufacturers make wonderful looking men's and women's shoes that combine good looks with comfort. Try to limit yourself to three pairs of shoes. I suggest bringing a formal shoe, walking shoe, and sandals or thongs. In all cases, search for versatile, multipurpose styles. For example, Rockport makes DresSport shoes that are appropriate for all but the most formal occasions. Teva or Clark sandals are also a walking shoe. Ecco Mobiles can be worn hiking and in the city, too. Other quality brands are Merrill, Timberland, SAS, and Easy Spirit.

Recommendations

The Walk Shop in Berkeley, California, which specializes in comfortable shoes, has a number of recommendations:

▼ All shoes should have springy, resilient composition soles that cushion the step as you walk. Leather is usually too hard. Injection molded soles form a permanent unit and are highly recommended.

▼ Look for thick or Vibram soles.

▼ Buy a shoe with an adjustable lace or strap because your foot changes size during the day. Slip-ons are better for short-term, rather than long-term, comfort.

▼ For tropical weather look for open styles that allow your feet to breathe.

▼ Some shoes, such as those made by Mephisto, Clark's, and Ecco, have "air conditioning," sophisticated airflow systems built into the sole to ventilate the foot.

▼ Some people need or wish to let their shoes dry completely between wearings. If you do, take an extra pair of shoes, or buy shoes such as those made by Ecco and Rockport, that come with removable insoles that can be taken out and dried between wearings. Instead of alternating shoes you can just change the insoles. Or buy Spenco removable insoles. For excessive perspiration, look for a lined shoe.

▼ Definitely take a pair of sandals for warm weather. Highly recommended are the three-strap, orthopedic-footbed sandal made by Clark's for women or the Teva for men and women. For men and women Reiker makes a design that is part shoe and part sandal, with a T-strap.

▼ Make sure your shoes are big enough and fit properly. Pay attention to the fit more than to the size.

▼ Make sure that you wear your shoes at least six or even twelve times before your trip. This gives you time to make necessary adjustments before you leave.

▼ Consider rain repellency. Many types of walking shoes are now made with waterproof leather. If you need to treat your shoes, get an alcohol-based treatment for general travel, such as Water Repellent Shield, an aerosol by Cadillac, not a silicone-based one. Silicone-based treatments seal the shoe completely and are recommended for hiking boots. Ultra Seal Waterproofing Boot Treatment Creme or Ultrathon Spray Boot Protection, both available at REI, are silicone-based. Both will darken the leather slightly as they provide protection against rain.

▼ Accessories

Accessories greatly extend the versatility of your travel wardrobe, enabling you to make a simple day outfit into dramatic evening attire. The travel wardrobe is a simple, classic background—accessories will add variety, texture, and color. They take up little room and will be a cheerful addition to your wardrobe.

SCARVES

- ▼ 1 large (at least 35 inches) square shawl. This is the most versatile shape and can be used to dress up a jacket, dress, or blouse. A shawl can be used as a head covering for religious sites, as an emergency blanket, and, in warm weather, will protect you from the sun or take the chill off in air-conditioned rooms.
- ▼ 1 long rectangle. Use it as a sash or with a blouse.
- ▼ 1 square (at least 25 inches square). A large bandana is a good all-purpose scarf.

BELTS

Take one or two in leather or fabric in neutral colors, or take high-quality elasticized belts with one or two interchangeable buckles. A snazzy metallic belt is useful for eveningwear. Covered buckles will match jewelry of any color. Fabric belts are appropriate for casual garments and warm climates.

JEWELRY

Keep it simple! Gold is universally appropriate, as are pearls for dress. Choose a few basic pieces: one pair of day earrings, one pair of evening earrings, costume pearls, and a simple gold chain. But if you love jewelry, here is where you can splurge. Do not take anything of monetary or sentimental value. It is not worth risking the loss. If you do, carry it in your security wallet and deposit it the hotel's safe deposit box. (But, see chapter 10 on security: not all hotels are trustworthy.)

BUTTON COVERS

Button covers, a new idea that is a boon to lightweight travelers, are jewelrylike decorations that come in sets of six and snap on over the regular buttons on shirts, sweaters, and jackets. They can transform a day garment for a glitzy evening out or just add pizazz when you are in the mood for a change.

SHOE CLIPS

Found in shoe departments, these clip-on decorations dress up pumps. Or you can use clip-on earrings.

HOSE

Plain stockings are the norm for business, but you can use color and texture to spice up your outfits for casual or evening wear. If you wear anything other than regular sizes, plan on taking enough hose from home to cover your trip. Take clear nail polish to stop runs.

PURSES/FANNY PACKS

Take one *small*, packable purse with a long shoulder strap. Select a simple and slightly elegant style that is also appropriate for a dressy evening. This is for your comb, tissues, pen, glasses, and a few dollars. You may also want to wear a fanny pack on a casual trip. For better security, get one that you can thread through your belt loops.

Important: Neither your purse nor your fanny pack should hold more than basic necessities such as notebook, pen, glasses, Kleenex, Chapstick, medications, and the like. A small amount of cash for the next few hours is all the money that you need. *All* your other valuables should *always* remain in your money belt.

▼ Making Your Packing List—Three Steps to Avoid "Just-in-Case" Syndrome

To avoid over- or under-packing, take the following three steps to focus on your wardrobe and travel-gear requirements for your trip.

Step 1. Research the Weather

Use your travel itinerary, a weather almanac such as the *International Traveler's Weather Guide* by Tom Loffman and Randy Mann (see Books in Resources), and the Itinerary Wardrobe Planner (see pages 80–81) to predict the temperature range, rain and humidity levels for your destinations. This will help you decide how many layers to bring and what types and weights of fabrics you will need. Pinpointing lodging and laundry facilities will clue you in on what fabrics will be maintainable and how many items of clothing you will need given your laundry schedule (i.e., staying at a bed-and-breakfast on a Sunday means you'll have to handwash, but London on a Monday means you'll be able to send out dry-cleaning).

Step 2. Analyze Your Activities

Use the Daily Activity Planner on page 82 to list clothing and gear needed each day for special events, sightseeing, outdoor and sports activities, and business meetings. Figure out in advance how you will create outfits for any special situations. Then use this information to complete your packing list.

Step 3. Make Your Packing List

Fill out the Women's Packing List on page 83 or Men's Packing List on page 84. Circle wardrobe items you need, then use this as a shopping list for any pieces needed to complete your wardrobe. When you pack the item, check it off. If it doesn't all fit in your suitcase, adjust your wardrobe and redo your list. Immediately after your trip, review the list and cross out items you didn't need for future reference. You can also use it as an inventory for insurance purposes should your belongings get lost. Whenever possible keep shopping receipts for this purpose.

▼ Itinerary Wardrobe Planner

Day No.	Date	Day of the week	Destination and type of lodging
1			
2			
3			
4			
5			
6			
7			
8			
9			
10			
11			
12			
13			
14			
15			
16			
17			
18			
19			
20			
21			
22			
23			
24			
25			
26			
27			
28			
29			
30			
31			

Weather Forecast				Laundry facilities
High	Low	Rain	Humidity	

▼ Daily Activity Planner

Day No.	Date	Location		
	Morning Activities	**Afternoon Activities**	**Evening Activities**	**Other Activities**
Layer 1 Underlayer				
Layer 2 Clothing				
Layer 3 Outerlayer				
Layer 4 Extremities; Shoes				
Accessories				
Gear				

▼ Women's Packing List

▼ Underlayer

- ☐ thermal underwear
- ☐ underpants
- ☐ bras
- ☐ garment shields
- ☐ hose, day
- ☐ hose, eve
- ☐ leggings/tights
- ☐ nightgown/big T-shirt
- ☐ swimsuit
- ☐ active wear
- ☐ pareo/sarong

▼ Clothing

- ☐ jacket #1
- ☐ jacket #2
- ☐ skirt #1
- ☐ skirt #2
- ☐ pants #1
- ☐ pants #2
- ☐ two-piece dress
- ☐ dress
- ☐ cardigan/sweater
- ☐ long-sleeved shirt
- ☐ shirt #2
- ☐ shirt #3
- ☐ shirt #4
- ☐ T-shirts
- ☐ shorts
- ☐ athletic, sport clothing
- ☐ other _____

▼ Outerlayer

- ☐ raincoat
- ☐ parka
- ☐ rainjacket
- ☐ rainpants
- ☐ windbreaker
- ☐ poncho
- ☐ umbrella

▼ Extremities

- ☐ shoes, dress
- ☐ shoes, walking
- ☐ sandals
- ☐ slippers
- ☐ socks, dress
- ☐ socks, casual
- ☐ sun hat
- ☐ rain hat
- ☐ ear warmer
- ☐ gloves/liners
- ☐ sock liners

▼ Accessories

- ☐ belts, day
- ☐ belts, evening
- ☐ bandana
- ☐ scarves
- ☐ handbag
- ☐ necklace
- ☐ pin
- ☐ earrings
- ☐ bracelets
- ☐ watch

▼ Men's Packing List

▼ Underlayer

- ☐ thermal underwear
- ☐ underpants
- ☐ undershirts
- ☐ big T-shirt
- ☐ pajamas
- ☐ swim trunks
- ☐ active wear
- ☐ pareo/sarong

▼ Clothing

- ☐ jacket #1
- ☐ jacket #2
- ☐ slacks #1
- ☐ slacks #2
- ☐ slacks #3
- ☐ vest
- ☐ sweater
- ☐ fleece jacket
- ☐ long-sleeved shirt
- ☐ shirt #2
- ☐ shirt #3
- ☐ shirt #4
- ☐ T-shirts
- ☐ shorts
- ☐ athletic, sport clothing
- ☐ other _____

▼ Outerlayer

- ☐ raincoat
- ☐ parka
- ☐ rainjacket
- ☐ rainpants
- ☐ windbreaker
- ☐ poncho
- ☐ umbrella

▼ Extremities

- ☐ shoes, dress
- ☐ shoes, walking
- ☐ sandals
- ☐ slippers
- ☐ socks, dress
- ☐ socks, casual
- ☐ sun hat
- ☐ rain hat
- ☐ ear warmer
- ☐ gloves/liners
- ☐ sock liners

▼ Accessories

- ☐ belts, day
- ☐ belts, evening
- ☐ bandana
- ☐ ties
- ☐ watch
- ☐ cufflinks

▼ Tips to Lighten the Load

- ▼ Wear your heaviest or bulkiest clothes on the plane.
- ▼ Take old underwear and socks and discard them as you go.
- ▼ Wear old walking shoes and discard them on the last day of your trip.
- ▼ Pack old clothes and give them away as you go to make room for souvenirs and new purchases.
- ▼ As a last resort, and to concentrate your resolve, pack your bag and walk a mile carrying it. If you can handle it, well and good. If it is too heavy, be ruthless.

5 | How to Pack Your Carry-on

In this chapter I will show you how to pack each of the basic carry-on pieces (one-, two-, and three-compartment bags and the convertible backpack) using the Bundle Method. I will also include details on packing accessories and offer tips on packing a garment bag and a secondary tote or daypack.

Important: Do *not* pack valuables such as passport, cash, credit cards, traveler's checks, tickets, extra photos, documents, and prescriptions. These go, *not* in your purse, your fanny pack, your carry-on, your briefcase or any other piece of luggage, but *on your person*, under your clothes, in a security wallet. No ifs, ands, or buts about it. (See pages 26–29.)

▼ The Bundle Method

The Bundle Method is a packing system perfect for soft-sided luggage. It creates a cushioned, woven mass of clothing (the bundle) that does not shift and hardly wrinkles. It is more versatile than rolling or folding because it accommodates tailored clothing, such as suits, skirts, slacks, and shirts or blouses as well as the more casual T-shirts and jeans. It can be used in any 45-inch carry-on, whether it is 20, 21, or 22 inches long and whether it has one, two, or three compartments. Used for the convertible backpack, the method may need to be modified to accommodate the body's center of gravity if you will be walking extensively.

Two key features make the bundle an asset for any traveler. First, it is a single unit of clothing that takes up the entire space in a 21- or 22-inch-long carry-on. In a completely filled case clothes move around less and are less likely to wrinkle. Second, the bundle has no sharp folds or creases, only soft, cushioned edges. The bundle is made up of layers of clothing wrapped around an inner cushion I call the core, which is a pouch containing lingerie, underwear, socks, and other accessories. Each item of clothing is cushioned; because there are no sharp creases, the clothes do not wrinkle.

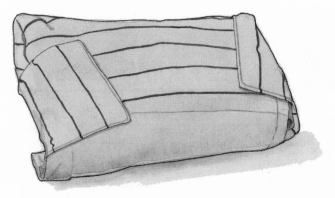

The bundle.

Before we pack anything, let's look at the bundle as it would appear after you have finished packing.

Packing It All In

Do not start packing until you have assembled every last item. Then read the directions for packing, right through, beginning with the next paragraph. There's more to packing than dumping stuff in a case and hoping you can shut the lid—but then you knew that, or you would not be reading this book. I will start with some general tips and then go on with detailed directions for packing the different items of clothing.

Always start with the largest, heaviest, and longest items of clothing, typically a jacket or dress, but not slacks. First pack tailored clothing that is likely to wrinkle. Save knits and wrinkle-resistant items such as sweaters for later.

Do not wrap anything in plastic—it is slippery and in the heat traps moisture, promoting wrinkling. You may use tissue paper to cushion folds if you wish. Long-lasting interfacing (Pellon) is another good material.

Place collars and waistbands alternately to create an even thickness of clothing.

Plan to use the wide dimension of the case for wide shoulders and wide skirts. The narrow dimension should be used for slacks, items folded in three (full dresses and skirts, A-line skirts), and other narrow items.

Before you begin, clear a space for packing, such as your bed or a clothing rack.

1. Put aside the clothing you will wear on the plane.

2. Make another pile of clothing and accessories you will want on arrival, for example, nightwear and slippers or a swimsuit.

3. Stack the rest of your wardrobe on the bed or hang on a clothes rack. If you are using a hanging clothes caddy, stack the garments as they are listed, from left to right; if you are using your bed, stack them from the bottom of the list up, so that item number one is on the top. Arrange as applicable:

WOMEN

1. Long *straight* skirt or *straight* dress
2. Jacket
3. Straight skirts
4. Dress—A-line or full skirted
5. Skirt—A-line or full
6. Slacks or split skirts
7. Shirts, long-sleeved (with scarf, if any)
8. Shirts, short-sleeved (with scarf, if any)
9. Sweater or other knits (if any)
10. Shorts

MEN

1. Jacket
2. Slacks
3. Shirts, long-sleeved
4. Shirts, short-sleeved
5. Sweater or other knits
6. Shorts

Also assemble the related underwear, socks, hose and other *wardrobe* accessories, including your swimsuit, which will be packed in your

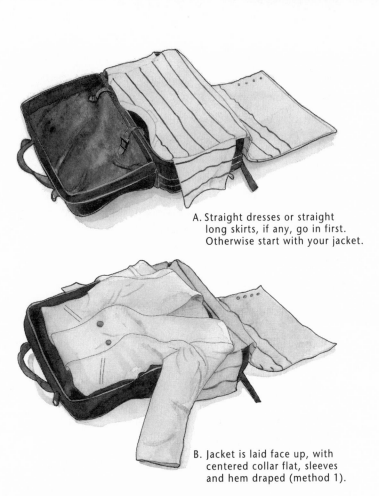

A. Straight dresses or straight long skirts, if any, go in first. Otherwise start with your jacket.

B. Jacket is laid face up, with centered collar flat, sleeves and hem draped (method 1).

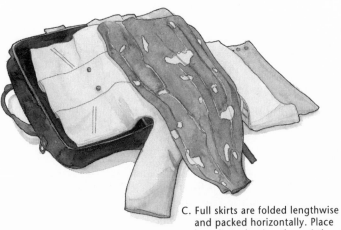

C. Full skirts are folded lengthwise and packed horizontally. Place hem first, draping the waistband.

core pouch (this is discussed below). Gather your shoe bags (your shoes stuffed with socks or hose), ties, and belts. Fold your travel raincoat and a small umbrella. Have your *travel* accessories on hand.

MAKING THE BUNDLE

Lay the suitcase on the bed. Open the deepest section completely so that the bag lies flat.

Straight dress or straight long skirt – (Illustration A.) For a straight dress, place the shoulders in the corners. Center the collar at the handle end of the case (top) so that the shoulders of the dress remain smooth. Make sure that the dress collar meets but does not bend against the wall of the bag.

Now, drape the bottom of the dress over the opposite end of the bag (where the hinge is). Drape the sleeves, if any, over the side walls of the bag. Smooth out the dress along the floor of the bag as best you can.

Jacket – This will make your first layer if you do not have a straight dress or long straight skirt. There are two ways to pack it:

Method 1: (Illustration B.) Button the jacket and lay it in the suitcase face up. The collar should lie flat, flush with but not bending up against, the hinge end of the case to allow the width of the collar and shoulders to remain smooth. Center the collar and hold it down using one hand. With the other hand, drape the bottom of the jacket over the handle (top) end of the bag. Drape the sleeves over the short sides of the bag. Use all of the space in the bag; get as close to the walls of the bag as possible.

Method 2: If the jacket is too wide or the sleeves do not drape easily, unbutton the jacket and lay it in the suitcase face down, with the collar flat. Bring in the lapels so that the width of the jacket fits the bag. Drape the bottom of the jacket over the handle (top) end of the bag. Bring the sleeves into the bag, laying them vertically down the jacket. Cushion the crease in the shoulder area if you wish. The fold will fall out quickly when the jacket is worn.

Straight skirts – Lay the skirt on top of the jacket, with the waistband at the *opposite edge* of the case from the jacket collar. Hold down the skirt with one hand and smooth it out with the other. Drape the

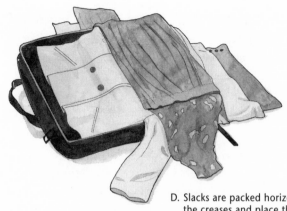

D. Slacks are packed horizontally. Match the creases and place the waistband along the edge, then smooth and drape.

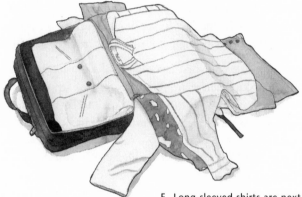

E. Long-sleeved shirts are next. Collars are face up; sleeves and hem are draped.

F. Short-sleeved shirts, T-shirts, and knits are next. Shorts and swimsuits are last. The core containing underwear is placed in the center.

bottom of the skirt over the opposite end of the bag. Add another skirt if desired, alternating waistbands.

A-line or full-skirted dress – Remember, full skirts are not to be recommended but, if you must take one, you will have to fold it in thirds before packing it. Lay the dress face down on a flat surface. Fold one side in, forming a straight vertical line. Fold the sleeve down vertically. Repeat for the other side. Now lay the dress in the bag horizontally, with the middle portion lying along the floor of the bag. Drape the shoulders over one side, the hem over the other.

A-line or full skirts – (Illustration C.) These, too, you will have to fold lengthwise and pack them using the horizontal direction of the bag. Lay the skirt on the bed. Fold in one side, a third, forming a straight vertical fold. Repeat on the opposite side. If you would like to cushion these folds, place some nylons, socks, or tissue paper in them to minimize the crease. Now, using the horizontal direction, lay the hem at one edge of the bag. Smooth the skirt, and drape the waistband over the opposite side. (Hems will wrinkle less if packed this way.)

Slacks – (Illustration D.) Match up both the creases in both legs. Center the slacks over the jacket (or skirts), leaving the waistband flush with the bag's narrow side. Smooth out the slacks and drape the bottoms over the opposite wall. If you have another pair, repeat the exercise, this time placing the waistband against the opposite edge.

Long-sleeved shirts – (Illustration E.) Lay shirts or blouses face up in the bag as you did the jacket, making sure to alternate collars. Make sure the collars are flat and not pushing up against the side of the bag. Drape the sleeves and bottoms over the sides.

Scarves – If you have scarves, pack them as a layer next to the blouse you might be wearing. (Similarly, once you are familiar with the technique, try putting whole outfits together.)

Short-sleeved shirts – (Illustration F.) Place them in the same way that you placed long-sleeved shirts. Lay them in the case, center the collar, drape the bottom and sides over the walls of the case.

Now you are finished with all of the wrinkle-prone, tailored items. You have also reached the center of the bundle. Here is where you put knits such as sweaters.

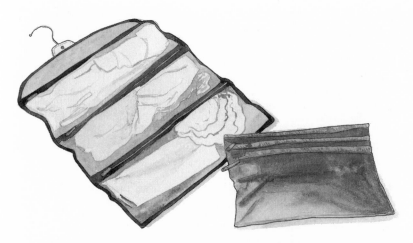

G. Samples of core pouches: these go in the middle of
your clothing bundle. For the organizer on the left,
tuck in hanger and fold pouch in half before packing.

H. Close the bundle by folding in sleeves and hems.
By smoothing as you go and packing tightly,
you will end up with fewer wrinkles in your clothes.

Sweater – Place your sweater or other knits over the blouses. Drape the bottom and sides.

Shorts – Where you place shorts depends upon their length. Match up both sets of seams. If they are very short, place them horizontally on top of the sweater. If they are walking length or are culottes, you will have to put them in after the slacks. Sometimes, depending where the hem falls, it also works better to use the wide dimension of the bag. Experiment with your shorts but place them as close to the middle of the bundle as possible.

Undershirts, boxer shorts, and sleepwear – These can be folded neatly and placed in the center of the space. Or place your sleepwear on top of the finished bundle so that it will be accessible upon arrival.

The core – (Illustration G.) The core acts as the center cushion, supporting the layers of clothing you have just put in. It is made up of a pouch (about 11 by 16 inches) containing your swimsuit and other wardrobe accessories such as lingerie, undergarments, socks, belt buckles, and so on. I recommend the Carry-rite Mini-organizer and the Deluxe Core Pouch (available at Easy Going—see Resources). Do not use a plastic resealable bag for the core: It is slippery and will cause garments to shift.

Place the core in the center of the bag with about two inches of space all around it. (Illustration F.) Make sure that the edges are nice and full—the better the edges are built up, the less wrinkling.

TO CLOSE THE BUNDLE

The core is covered by layers of the clothing that you draped over the sides of the bag. Fold back the bottom of the garment that was layered immediately below the core. (Illustration H.) Then fold the sleeve across the core, wrapping any extra material around the curve of the core. Repeat for the other sleeve. (Illustration I.) Continue down through the layers, wrapping each around the core and smoothing out wrinkles. (Illustration J.) Pack as tightly as you can. Make sure you fold the bottom of the garment up first and then each sleeve; do not interweave garments with one another.

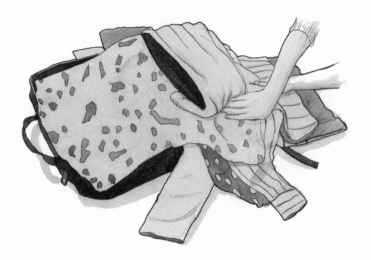

I. Tuck sleeves around the core; this cushions the folds and prevents sharp creases.

J. Fold hems around the core; continue with each layer.

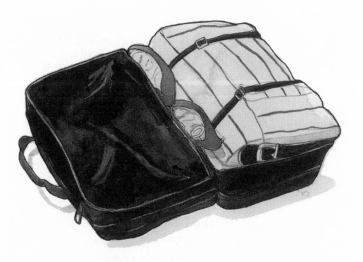

K. The finished bundle. Place shoes along bottom
edge of bag; tuck belt around the zippered rim.

After the last layer is folded over, secure the tie straps to keep your wardrobe in place. Do not cinch them too tightly.

Shoes – You have space for one pair of shoes in this section and one in the other section. Place shoe bags along the bottom of the case next to the bundle. If they are flat, place the heels in the corners of the bag with soles facing the hinge. (Illustration K.) Place high heels diagonally inward. The heel should not face the hinge or the clothing. If you have large shoes, try placing them with the toes at an angle or cut down on the number of pairs you take, use accessory space, or that second totebag.

Belts – Place belts along the inside zippered rim of the suitcase (Illustration K.).

Ties – Can be handled a number of ways. If you want nice, crisp ties, buy a tie case that fits the measurements of the bag, and lay it on top of the bundle. You can also use a stiff piece of cardboard and wrap the ties around it, securing them with a rubber band. Or, for those ties you *might* use if you get into that four-star restaurant in Paris, simply wrap them around the finished bundle.

Accessible items – Lay items you want access to immediately neatly on top of the bundle or tucked in the corners. Such items might include the next day's socks and underwear, a folded nightgown, a swimsuit, or a sweater.

SHORT CUTS

Sometimes lack of time, impatience, or anxiety about customs creates the desire for a slightly faster method of packing, even if slightly more wrinkling may occur. There are ways to simplify the procedure and two other ways of assembling a bundle. Experiment with them and see if you like them better.

Alternative packing method 1 – Lay all the items in the suitcase, with collars and waistbands stacked in the same direction. Drape all sides as you would if you were using the perfectionist's method. Place the core in the middle. Now take all the bottoms at once and fold them over the core. Then take all the right sleeves at once and fold them over the core, wrapping them around if need be. Do the same with the left sleeves. Voila! There is your bundle. The difference is that the outer edges are not as nicely built and the sides of the garments will wrinkle. But, if you are in a hurry or on your way home, who cares?

Alternative packing method 2 – This method makes access a little easier, because you can pull individual outfits out. But it makes for less cushioning and more wrinkling as each outfit is packed in a separate bundle.

To make each bundle, lay an entire outfit in together as you plan to wear it. For example, lay in the jacket, slacks, blouse, and scarf, and perhaps sweater, that you want to wear tomorrow. Drape all sides. Place core objects, such as your underwear, socks, bra, and so on in the middle. Now close up the bundle. Pack your next outfit the same way, until all your clothing is in. Save items that you will be wanting immediately when you unpack, such as pajamas or nightgown, on top of the bundles.

Unpacking

When you arrive at your hotel, unfurl the bundle and let the garments drape over the sides of the bag. This will give them a chance to breathe and rest. Hang them up if you will be staying a few days. You will find it is easy to insert the hangers while the clothes are still in the bag. To repack, you will not have to fold much, just lay the garments in quickly. Nor will you have to iron, so you will save even more time in the long run.

GETTING CLOTHES IN AND OUT

If you have packed only separates, it is easy to unfurl two or three garments, reach inside the bundle to grab the one you need, slip it out, and repack. If you have packed longer items such as a dress, you will have more to unwrap. This is another reason for packing separates only!

▼ Packing a Three-Compartment Carry-on with Two Wardrobes

These instructions that follow are for packing a 21-inch or 22-inch-long bag that has three full-length compartments. This configuration is the most convenient for multipurpose and multiclimate trips because it allows you to organize your clothing according to purpose and season. The deepest section will hold your wardrobe bundle for business and cold weather, the second will hold a minimalist leisure and warm-weather wardrobe, the third contains all your other accessories. Note: You need a core pouch for each separate bundle.

Section 1

Make a bundle with your dress or cold-weather clothes. Put the bundle in the deepest section of the bag.

Section 2

This compartment will hold casual or warm-weather items, if applicable. When you have a second wardrobe make a separate bundle, arranging your casual jacket, skirts, slacks, long-sleeve shirt, T-shirts, and walking shorts in that order. Assemble the related underwear, socks, and other wardrobe accessories in the core pouch.

Section 3

This compartment will hold all your other accessories, everything that is not part of your wardrobe. Use this compartment for your packable raincoat and umbrella, toiletry kit or dopp kit, laundry kit, medical kit, collapsible bag, Packtowl, hairdryer, iron or steamer, water purification needs, flask, packable purse or fanny pack (stuffed with odds and ends such as immersion heater, money exchange calculator, and so on), books and maps, converter and adapters. Think of this space as four or five vertical columns, running from the bottom hinge to the top. This is an efficient use of the space.

Pack the columns in stacks from front to back, with flat items toward the middle and irregular shapes toward the outside. Pack all the heavy items at the bottom of the bag, with light objects on top. Because your toiletry or shave kit is fourteen or fifteen inches high, it will stand in the suitcase vertically. Your packable raincoat and umbrella go here. Cushion objects such as hairdryers with the raincoat.

▼ Packing a Three-Compartment Carry-on with One Wardrobe

If you have only one basic wardrobe, you will probably be able to fit all the garments in the middle section of the bag. This gives you lots of flexibility for using the other two side pockets. In one side compartment put your accessories. In the other you can put your dirty laundry, clothing (such as a sweater) or items you want quick access to, extra shoes, or business papers.

▼ Packing a One-Compartment Carry-on

Pullman cases, wheeled luggage, and other rigid bags have only one deep section. Some include a partition, making it a two-compartment bag. The best way to pack such bags is in three layers: a bottom layer made up of your accessories, irregularly shaped objects, and shoes; a middle layer made up of the bundle, and a top layer of anything you want access to immediately on arrival or during your flight.

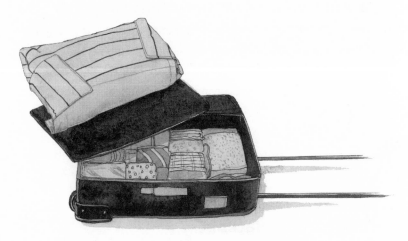

One-compartment bag, with accessories
in bottom, then partition, then bundle.

1. On the bottom of the bag, place your travel gear: toiletry kit, laundry kit, appliances, and so on (see illustration above). Shoes can go here, too, placed near the bottom hinge of the bag. Do not wrap things in plastic—it is slippery and will cause objects to shift in the case as it is handled. You will probably fill the entire space. If you do not, add rolled-up socks, T-shirts, and other soft garments to fill gaps and prevent items from moving.

   Hint: To keep the accessories from moving about and create a smooth surface for packing the bundle, buy a package of light- to medium-weight nonwoven interfacing (the brand name is Pellon) at a fabric store. Each piece is 3 yards long by 22 inches wide. Cut a piece double the length of your suitcase and fold it in half. Lay it over the accessories, in effect creating a sectional divider. Tuck the edges down around the sides of the bag, enclosing the accessories and creating a shelf.

2. Make your bundle as described on pages 87–97.

3. Lay whatever you want immediate access to on top of the bundle.

▼ Packing a Two-Compartment Carry-on

For the two-compartment suitcase you do not need to make a divider. Typically the bag has a partition for organizing contents into separate compartments and is most suitable for a single-bundle wardrobe.

1. Pack section one, the bottom side, with accessories, irregular objects, and shoes as you would the one-compartment bag.

2. Pack section two, the top side, with the bundle and shoes.

3. Lay whatever you want access to on top of the bundle. Tuck socks and underwear in the corners of the bag.

▼ Packing a Travel Pack (Convertible Backpack)

Travel packs require a different technique because, if you are doing serious walking, you have to take weight distribution into consideration. Heavy items should be carried lower and closer to your body. Lighter items should be packed away from your back. Also, the bundle is packed beneath the accessories and lies against your back. Be careful not to underpack. Use the outer cinch straps to help keep the pack balanced and items in place. The bag will usually contain your clothing, accessories, shoes, and there are two ways to pack a convertible pack for general travel: the Bundle Method and the roll-and-stuff method.

Bundle method –

1. Make a bundle of your clothes, keeping aside what you want quick access to (a sweater, and so on). Lay the bundle in the well of the bag and secure it with tie straps.

2. Nest one shoe inside the other and place the pair along the bottom edge of the bag. (If you are carrying your bag vertically, this will be near the waistbelt.)

3. Place accessories on top of and around the bundle, using organizers such as stuff sacks, nylon pouches, and Ziploc bags. Heavier items should be clustered toward the bottom edge.

4. Items you need to reach quickly place on top of the accessories, near the zippers, or in outside pockets.

Roll-and-stuff method – If you are carrying the backpack all day, you may want to redistribute the weight. Roll your clothes and place them in stuff sacks, one each for clean clothes, dirty clothes, city clothes, hiking clothes, and so on. Accessories can go in pouches, stuff sacks, or Ziploc bags. Place lighter items such as the clothing sacks higher and farther from your back, and heavier items lower and closer to your back. Items you need to retrieve quickly should be placed around the edges and in outside pockets.

▼ Packing a Garment Bag

Layer between two and four items on a single sturdy hanger. Start with a sweater and cover it with a shirt and a jacket, so that each layer, including sleeves, will cushion the next. Drape slacks on the hanger bar over other items such as skirts.

Long plastic dry-cleaning bags can be put over clothes to help minimize wrinkles.

Pack the hangers holding easily wrinkled items such as blouses and shirts toward the back of the bag to cushion the horizontal crease when the bag is folded in half.

As soon as you arrive at the hotel, hang up your clothes, each garment on a separate hanger.

▼ Packing a Totebag or Daypack

Keep in mind the sequence of your needs when packing your day-pack. To avoid losing items try to return them to their proper place.

Outside pockets –

- ▼ Boarding passes, customs documents, local currency, and any other items you need accessible for boarding and leaving the plane or train
- ▼ Pen and notebook
- ▼ Emergency items: knife, flashlight, and so on
- ▼ Toiletries: moist towelettes, toilet-seat covers, tampons, mints, toothbrush and toothpaste, comb, lip balm, moisturizer, headache reliever
- ▼ Snack

On top near the zipper –

▼ Medicine, cup, water bottle; eyeglasses, sunglasses

▼ Inflight materials: business papers, reading materials, cassette player, maps, guidebook, and so on

▼ Thick socks for the plane

Bottom – At the bottom place valuables, clothing, and other necessities you will not need frequently.

▼ Sweater or jacket, umbrella, keys, camera and film, half of your traveler's checks, a change of clothing

6 Business Travel

For business people, carry-on luggage has many benefits. It gives you more control over your trip and schedule by eliminating the possibility of lost luggage and allowing you to avoid the carousel and get right to your hotel or meeting. Traveling light and remaining mobile with your hands free also enables you to make phone calls and write easily. Mobility also reduces the risk of becoming a target for pickpockets and thieves while standing around waiting for luggage at crowded airports.

I recommend your taking one or two carry-ons that you can handle easily yourself. They should all have shoulder straps or wheels (either built-in or on a wheeled luggage cart). You should be able to lift them easily into the overhead bin.

For the following wardrobes, I recommend the Bundle Method of packing in a three-compartment, 21-inch-long semisoft shoulder bag. This gives you maximum flexibility in organizing your wardrobe. It accommodates a jacket quite well. If you prefer, use a garment bag and still go carry-on but keep in mind that a heavily laden garment bag can be unwieldy and difficult to manage, particularly if you are small. It will be easier to balance your load between two lighter bags and pack an extra suit or evening dress in a garment cover that has no pockets.

For short trips with a minimalist or moderate wardrobe (one jacket) you might consider:

▼ 1 three-compartment carry-on suitcase with shoulder straps plus a shoulder totebag or daypack (put your briefcase or notebook computer inside the tote for security)

▼ A garment bag with pockets plus a totebag or briefcase

▼ A wheel-aboard carry-on with retractable handle and hook for an extra totebag, plus a totebag or briefcase

For longer trips or a luxury wardrobe, you might consider:

- ▼ 1 three-compartment carry-on, a simple lightweight garment cover for a suit or dresses, and a luggage cart with a garment-bag-attachment hook
- ▼ A single capacious garment bag with pockets plus a shoulder tote for your briefcase

▼ Traveling with a Portable Computer

There are three types of portable computers: laptops, notebooks, and subnotebooks. Laptops weigh around twelve pounds, notebooks six pounds, and the new subnotebooks three pounds. Add to these the printer, extra battery, charger, cabling, and disks to determine the load you will have to carry.

It pays to invest in the lightweight versions. Some models combine a computer with a printer, and weigh only seven and a half pounds. To avoid carrying the printer, you might arrange to use your disk in a larger computer at your destination.

Most models have dual-voltage converters; you will still need the proper adapter plug for the wall sockets. You can buy adapter plugs with or without grounding pins. If you are traveling with a modem, phone jack adapters for use on foreign phone outlets are available from Aris Export (see Resources). An extension cord may be useful.

Pack your computer in a well-padded softsided bag that protects it against breakage. There are many totebags designed to handle a portable computer, its accessories, and some personal items. Pack some extra batteries; airport prices are very high.

For international travel, preregister a foreign-made model with the U.S. Customs Service on Form 4457. You will need to describe it and list the serial number. U.S.-made computers should present no problem at customs. For any computer, carry the sales receipt and appropriate export/import declaration form with you.

Avoid putting disks and computer through the metal detector, as they can be ruined. Put the equipment on the conveyor belt. X-rays cannot affect disks and computer equipment.

Companies such as Tenba and Haliburton specialize in appropriate softsided and metal shipping cases for photographic, computer, or trade show equipment to be checked through. Remin Kart-a-Bag makes specialty luggage carts for travelers who are carrying such equipment through.

▼ The Business Travel Wardrobe

Traveling for business requires a careful focus. Your wardrobe must be consistent with your professional environment and career image. If you are moving around a great deal and meeting with different people, you can take the minimalist wardrobe, laundering as you go. If you will be seeing the same people constantly, you will require the moderate or luxury wardrobes. You may find a second bag or hanging-suit bag necessary.

Here are a few guidelines for putting together a business wardrobe:

- ▼ Research the dress code for your destination. This can differ tremendously by state and country.

- ▼ Research climate and activities—these will dictate your wardrobe needs. Do not take more than you will need.

- ▼ Pack simple, classic styles. Err on the conservative side. Follow the dress code for your company and career image, even if events are off-site or casual.

- ▼ Dress and casual wear should be interchangeable whenever possible. Men should pack a suit jacket and slacks that match or can be worn casually. A suit with two pairs of matching slacks is also a good idea.

- ▼ Stick to two coordinating neutrals. Make one a dark neutral that will be suitable for day and evening—black, navy, gray, or brown. The second should be a lighter coordinating color such as white, ivory, or khaki. Use accent colors, such as burgundy, red, and other brights, for shirts and blouses. (See the color charts on page 61). Shoes, belts, and handbags should be in your basic neutral colors.

- ▼ Pack lighter colors and looser styles in warmer climates, using natural fibers and natural blends—they breathe better. Men's business shirts should be long-sleeved in lighter weights.

- ▼ Pack darker colors for cooler climates, using wool gabardine and worsted wools for suit pieces.
- ▼ Pack thermal silk underwear in suitable styles for cold weather.
- ▼ Do not feel that you must pack scarves. Take them only if you are comfortable tying and wearing them.
- ▼ Keep a sweater accessible on the plane in case it is chilly. Also keep an extra blouse or shirt, underpants, and socks or hose in your carry-on if you have to check your luggage through for any reason.

▼ Women's Business Travel Wardrobes

Business Suit Wardrobe for Women

This wardrobe is for the woman who wears suits during the day and has special dinners or other events in the evening.

MINIMALIST

Layer 1 – Underlayer

- ▼ 3–6 pairs of underpants (3 if you will wash, 6 if not)
- ▼ 2 bras
- ▼ 1–2 sets of garment shields
- ▼ Silk knit undershirt or camisole to wear under blouses if cold
- ▼ Above-the-knee silk shorties to wear under skirts if cold
- ▼ 1 half-slip (optional)
- ▼ 1 extra-large T-shirt or coverup, for sleepwear, pool *or* pajamas *or* nightgown
- ▼ Bathing suit with cover-up (optional)

Layer 2 – Clothing

- ▼ 1 suit
- ▼ 2 blouses (both day-into-evening)

▼ 1 two-piece dress that coordinates with the suit *or* 1 simple shirtwaist dress in a coordinating neutral tone

Layer 3 – Outerlayer

▼ 1 raincoat and umbrella, if needed

Layer 4 – Extremities

▼ 1 pair of walking pumps

▼ 1 pair of dress pumps for evening

▼ 3 pairs of hose, for day (more if you don't want to wash)

▼ 2 pairs of hose for evening (sheer)

▼ Thongs for pool, if needed

▼ Athletic shoes or sneakers, if needed

▼ Athletic clothing and underwear, if needed

Accessories

▼ 2 scarves

▼ Jewelry (earrings, brooch, chains)

▼ 1 evening handbag

MODERATE

To the minimalist wardrobe add:

▼ 1 suit

▼ 1 blouse

LUXURY

To the moderate wardrobe add:

▼ 1 two-piece dress *or* other dress, for evening wear

▼ 1 pair of evening shoes

▼ Accessories for evening wear

Business Coordinates Wardrobe for Women

Classic-looking coordinates are for women who do not need business suits but must look professional. All items should be day-into-evening styles. Pack the Business Suit Wardrobe (above), with the following substitutions:

Layer 2 – Clothing

▼ 1 simple jacket (unstructured type)

▼ 1 skirt, tailored style (*or* 1 pair of slacks)

▼ 1 two-piece dress *or* 1 chemise-type or shirtwaist dress

▼ 1 or 2 blouses (one for day or evening)

Layer 4 – Extremities

▼ 3 scarves (1 shawl, 1 long rectangular, 1 square) (optional)

▼ Simple jewelry (gold, pearls, chains)

▼ 1 or 2 leather belts

▼ Day handbag (or use briefcase)

▼ Small shoulder bag for day or evening

▼ 3 pairs of hose, for day (more if you don't want to wash)

▼ 2 pairs of hose, for evening (sheer)

▼ 1 pair of walking pumps in a neutral color

▼ 1 pair of pumps for evening, if needed

▼ Thongs for pool, if needed

MODERATE

To the minimalist wardrobe add:

▼ 1 skirt *or* 1 pair of slacks

▼ 1 cardigan sweater (V-neck, to wear alone and with others)

LUXURY

For special events, to the moderate wardrobe add:

▼ 1 dress

▼ 1 pair of shoes for a special outfit

▼ Accessories for a special outfit

Combined Business and Leisure Wardrobe for Women

Clothes for casual activities after your business trip are easily included in your carry-on bag. If you are on the move and need room in your suitcase, send your suits home by Federal Express or UPS after the meetings are over.

To the minimalist business wardrobes listed above add the following for casual wear.

▼ 1 pair of casual slacks

▼ 1 pair of knee-length shorts (optional)

▼ 1 skirt (optional)

▼ 2 casual shirts, such as a matching blouse and tank top

▼ 1 pair of athletic or walking shoes

▼ 2 or 3 sets of casual socks

▼ Active wear for golf, tennis, and so on, as needed

Off-site Business and Casual Wardrobe for Women

Sometimes, at a week-long conference held at a resort, there will be business seminars or meetings during the day, dressier events at night, and a company barbecue at the weekend. This is the hardest trip to plan for because you need clothes for a variety of situations. You will be seeing the same people every day, so you will probably want to take a few more clothes. Casual in such settings does not mean T-shirt and jeans; wardrobe protocol must still be observed. Your best-looking casual clothing should be carefully chosen. If you wear the suit or casual outfit on the plane, you should be able to pack this entire wardrobe (which is in a black, khaki, and burgundy color scheme) in one carry-on suitcase and a shoulder bag. Or, if you prefer, use a garment bag. For this wardrobe, pack the Business Suit Wardrobe (pages 108–109), with the following substitutions:

Layer 2 – Clothing

▼ 1 jacket and skirt *or* a suit, black (for day meetings and evening)

▼ 1 skirt, khaki

- ▼ 1 pair of black silk slacks, for evening
- ▼ 1 plain cream-colored blouse (day or evening)
- ▼ 1 burgundy blouse (day or evening)
- ▼ 1 two-piece dress in a print, black and khaki (or black, khaki, and burgundy if you can find it) *or* one shirtwaist dress (day or evening)
- ▼ 1 burgundy cardigan or sweater set
- ▼ 1 pair of khaki slacks (for the barbecue)
- ▼ 1 casual top (for the barbecue) (can be one half of the sweater set)

Layer 3 – Outerlayer

- ▼ 1 windbreaker, if needed

Layer 4 – Extremities

- ▼ 2 pairs of casual socks
- ▼ 1 burgundy belt
- ▼ 1 pair of black pumps (business)
- ▼ 1 pair of burgundy loafers *or* oxford-type shoes (for the barbecue)
- ▼ Thongs *or* light sandals for the pool, if needed

Accessories

- ▼ 3 scarves (1 shawl, 1 long rectangular, 1 square) (optional)
- ▼ Simple jewelry (gold, pearls, chains)
- ▼ Day handbag
- ▼ Small shoulder bag for evening
- ▼ 3 pairs of hose, for day (more if you don't want to wash)
- ▼ 2 pairs of hose, for evening (sheer)

▼ Men's Business Travel Wardrobes

Regular Business Wardrobe for Men

If you will be meeting with different people everyday, you can keep your clothing to a minimum. If you are with the same people constantly, you will need a few more shirts and a second suit.

MINIMALIST

Layer 1 – Underlayer

- 3–8 pairs of undershorts
- Silk knit thermal undershirt and bottoms to wear if cold
- 1 extra-large T-shirt for coverup and sleepwear, *or* 1 pair of pajamas
- Swim trunks, if needed

Layer 2 – Clothing

- 1 suit
- 1 pair of matching slacks (to double as casual wear)
- 3–5 dress shirts (3 if you send laundry out or take 1 shirt for each business day)
- 1 or 2 casual shirts, such as polo-type

Layer 3 – Outerlayer

- 1 raincoat and umbrella, if needed

Layer 4 – Extremities

- 3–5 pairs of dress socks (1 for each day of the trip)
- 2 ties *or* 1 tie for each day of the trip
- 1 belt
- 1 pair of dress shoes
- 1 pair of athletic shoes, if needed
- Athletic clothing (T-shirt, shorts, underwear, socks, nylon warm-up suit), if needed

MODERATE

For trips of one week or more, to the minimalist wardrobe add:

- 1 suit or a blazer

LUXURY

If you are planning to take a garment bag, to the moderate wardrobe add:

- 1 suit *or* tuxedo

Combined Business and Casual Wardrobe for Men

Try using patterned socks, motif ties, a patterned sweater, or sports shirts to bring variety into the wardrobe, which is based on a color scheme.

Layer 1 – Underlayer

- ▼ 3–8 pairs of undershorts
- ▼ Silk knit thermal undershirt and bottoms, if cold
- ▼ 1 extra-large T-shirt for coverup and sleepwear, *or* 1 pair of pajamas
- ▼ Swim trunks, if needed

Layer 2 – Clothing

- ▼ 1 dark suit (optional in some settings)
- ▼ 1 navy blazer
- ▼ 1 dress shirt for each business day (at least one white) with ties
- ▼ 2 pairs of slacks, 1 gray, 1 khaki (the latter doubles as casual)
- ▼ 1 pullover or cardigan sweater (cordovan V- or crew-neck, print or pattern)
- ▼ 2 casual shirts (striped, patterned, or polo-type)

Layer 3 – Outerlayer

- ▼ 1 raincoat *or* windbreaker and umbrella

Layer 4 – Extremities

- ▼ 5 pairs of dress socks (or 1 for each day of trip if not washing)
- ▼ 1 belt, black
- ▼ 1 pair of dress shoes, black
- ▼ 1 pair of casual loafers or oxfords, cordovan
- ▼ Thongs for pool, if needed
- ▼ Athletic clothing (underwear, socks, and shoes), if needed
- ▼ Cufflinks, tie clips, other accessories as needed

▼ Security

Travelers on business can be targets for theft and terrorist crimes. If you are traveling internationally, it pays to avoid being identified as a business traveler. Carry inconspicuous softsided luggage. Briefcases and computers should be put into your nylon expandable tote, in a daypack, or in your suitcase. Pack your backup disks separately from the computer for extra security. For more about the subject, see chapter 10.

▼ Checklist for Business Travel

- ☐ security wallet and contents (see pages 26–29)
- ☐ attache case
- ☐ business cards
- ☐ calculator
- ☐ expense ledger
- ☐ personal organizer: appointments, schedule, addresses and phone numbers, calendar
- ☐ business papers/files
- ☐ itinerary
- ☐ frequent flyer/rental car/discount/gym membership vouchers and cards
- ☐ confirmations and vouchers
- ☐ convention pre-registration and name tags
- ☐ notepad/pen/business stationery/ envelopes
- ☐ other office supplies (see pages 43–44)
- ☐ computer equipment (see page 44)
- ☐ other _____
- ☐ other _____

7 | Adventure Travel and Active Vacations

Bags packed for physcially active vacations are far more likely to contain stuff taken "just in case" than are those packed for business travel, when the agenda is set in advance and amenities are readily available. Packing for an adventure trip or active vacation requires you to balance self-sufficiency against the need to travel light. The need for self-sufficiency increases if you travel in areas where such things as medications and clean water are not available. Also, you must be prepared for various microclimates (such as those of jungle basins or mountaintops) during a single trip. Then, if your itinerary includes visits to cities, you will need "civilized" clothing as well.

In this chapter I outline a Basic Adventure Wardrobe with weather adjustments for cold, trekking/high altitude, wet/humid, and dry/desert climates. Fast-drying, high-performance clothing is mandatory, since active vacations bring one face-to-face with the elements and produce lots of laundry, too. A basic travel gear checklist is also included. For conventional trips, such as leisure, sightseeing vacations, and long weekends, refer to the Basic Carry-on Wardrobe in chapter 4 (pages 52–57) as your starting point.

▼ Women's Basic Adventure Wardrobe

This wardrobe is suitable for any warm-weather on-your-own trip. If cool weather is expected, select heavier fabrics and follow suggestions in Adjusting for Weather (starting on page 120).

MINIMALIST

Layer 1 – Underlayer

- ▼ 2 or 3 T-shirts
- ▼ 4 pairs of underpants

- ▼ 2 bras
- ▼ 1 pareo or sarong *or* large T-shirt (for sleeping, lounging, and cover-up)
- ▼ 1 bathing suit (one-piece)

Layer 2 – Clothing

- ▼ 1 lightweight cardigan
- ▼ 2 long-sleeved shirts
- ▼ 1 pair of slacks (cool, comfortable, loose-fitting; often sold as "hiking pants")
- ▼ 2 travel skirts, mid-length, lightweight cotton or cotton/polyester blend with pockets
- ▼ 1 pair of walking shorts, knee-length, with pockets

Layer 3 – Outerlayer

- ▼ 1 lightweight raincoat, nylon poncho, or windbreaker, with hood

Layer 4 – Extremities

- ▼ 1 pair of walking shoes—these can be running shoes or lightweight walking shoes, which can be worn around camp, walking in the rain forest and in the city, or sturdy walking sandals; if you want a closed shoe for hiking in jungles or rivers, you will need a second pair of walking shoes that can get wet
- ▼ 1 pair of sturdy sandals—these can be "super sandals," such as Tevas if you plan to be in rivers, reefs, beaches, or other wet places; otherwise, Clark's orthopedic sandals are great
- ▼ 1 pair of canvas shoes (espadrilles) *or* light sandals for dress (optional)
- ▼ 4 pairs of lightweight socks (such as sock liners) in polyester (e.g., Capilene) or a silk knit
- ▼ 2 bandanas, 1 large for sun protection
- ▼ Hat—for sun, take a wide-brimmed sun hat, preferably one that will protect your neck and ears; a baseball cap is also fine; just be sure to use sunscreen

MODERATE

To the minimalist wardrobe add:

- ▼ 1 outfit for the city: short-sleeved camp shirt and skirt *or* a cool shirtdress
- ▼ 1 T-shirt
- ▼ Sashes, belts
- ▼ Jewelry, simple beads and earrings
- ▼ 1 pair of espadrilles or sandals for the city

LUXURY

To the moderate wardrobe add:

- ▼ 1 outfit for the city

This will probably push you over the edge for carry-on; avoid it if possible.

▼ Men's Basic Adventure Wardrobe

This wardrobe is suitable for any warm-weather trip. See guidelines for cool-weather changes, starting on page 120.

MINIMALIST

Layer 1 – Underlayer

- ▼ 2 T-shirts (polo-style)
- ▼ 4 pairs of underpants
- ▼ 1 pair of swim trunks (shorts can double as trunks)
- ▼ 1 pareo or sarong or large T-shirt (for sleeping, lounging, and cover-up)

Layer 2 – Clothing

- ▼ 1 lightweight sweater
- ▼ 2 long-sleeved shirts, with pockets
- ▼ 2 pairs of slacks with pockets (cool, comfortable, loose-fitting trousers; those sold as "hiking pants," with lots of pockets, are good)

▼ 1 pair of walking shorts, knee-length, with pockets

Layer 3 – Outerlayer

▼ 1 lightweight nylon poncho or windbreaker, with hood

Layer 4 – Extremities

▼ 1 pair of walking shoes—running shoes or other walking shoes that can be worn around camp, in town, and walking in the rain forest; if you want a closed shoe for hiking in jungles or rivers, you will need a second pair of walking shoes that can get wet.

▼ 1 pair of sturdy sandals or thongs—these should be "super sandals" such as Tevas, if you plan to be in rivers, reefs, beaches, or other wet places; otherwise any open, comfortable shoe is fine.

▼ 4 pairs of lightweight socks (such as sock liners) in polypropylene, Capilene, silk, or other synthetic

▼ 2 bandanas, 1 large

▼ Hat—for sun, take a wide-brimmed sun hat, preferably one that protects neck and ears; a baseball cap is fine; just use sunscreen.

MODERATE

To the minimalist wardrobe add:

▼ 1 jacket

LUXURY

To the moderate wardrobe add:

▼ 1 outfit for the city (slacks and shirt)

This will probably push you over the edge for one carry-on; avoid it if at all possible.

▼ Adjusting for Weather, Climate, and Type of Trip

You may need to adjust the fabrics, number of layers, and shoes depending on the conditions of your trip. Consider the following suggestions in selecting your adventure wardrobe.

Cold-Weather Travel

▼ Take a pair of warm wool socks

▼ Add underpants as they will dry more slowly

▼ Add thermal long underwear or cotton tights or leggings

▼ Substitute a pair of heavier weight slacks for the shorts

▼ Take a cotton turtleneck instead of a T-shirt

▼ Substitute a wool button-down long-sleeved shirt or pullover for the light long-sleeved shirt

▼ Substitute a fleece jacket for the cardigan

▼ Pack warm shoes instead of open shoes

▼ Add a warm hat and gloves

Trekking or High-Altitude Travel

If your trip includes a trek to high altitudes, add the following to the adventure wardrobe. Try to rent most equipment and heavy clothing at your destination.

▼ Long underwear (medium-weight)

▼ A down parka or vest (rent it at your destination if possible)

▼ A Polarfleece jacket

▼ Watertight raingear

▼ Lightweight weather-sealed hiking boots (do *not* rent these; wear them on the plane to save suitcase space)

▼ For the tropics take ankle-height, nylon hiking boots with removable insoles, or light, weather-sealed leather boots

▼ 2 pairs of thick quick-drying socks, such as polypropylene

▼ Wool hat

▼ Mittens or gloves (optional)

▼ Sneakers

Tropical Travel

Humidity, hot sun, periodic rain, and cold at high altitudes are marks of the tropics. You need high-performance outdoor gear that dries quickly. Sunscreen, lip balm, mosquito repellent or netting, and anti-itch remedies are essential.

For tropical travel, take the Adventure Wardrobe and follow these guidelines:

CLOTHING

Choose garments that are loose-fitting in a weave that helps ventilate the body. T-shirts should be of 100 percent cotton or a cotton/polyester blend. Mesh polo-type T-shirts are good because they protect the neck from the sun and are more versatile than plain T-shirts are. Long-sleeved shirts can be of cotton/polyester blends. (A combination of 65 percent polyester and 35 percent cotton makes a good fabric; Patagonia makes one called "Fishing Gear"; another, "The Baja Shirt," is available from TravelSmith. Patagonia also makes an A/C line of clothing especially for humid weather.)

Ideally skirts, slacks, and sport jackets can be of easy-care fabrics made of polyester/cotton, cotton/nylon, or tropical weight wool/polyester blends. Spandex gives clothing an added measure of comfort. Women may want to bring a cool shirtdress for citywear. Underwear should be of quick-drying synthetics or synthetic blends. Shorts are not acceptable in all areas—check before packing them. You may want to consider a conservative, knee-length style with lots of pockets in a quick-drying cotton/nylon blend. Take a sun hat and chiffon scarves or bandannas to keep the hair off your head. If you have time to shop, hats, scarves, and sarongs will often be available at your destination. Plan on washing one item while the second dries, and buy everything in fast-drying fabrics.

Note: In Asia and Moslem countries, women's wardrobes should be modest.

SHOES

In humid climates shoes will get very sweaty and heavy. Mildew is a constant threat. It may be slightly harder to consolidate and wear the same shoes all the time. Try to limit yourself to three pairs of shoes.

If you are going to be in wet places such as rivers, jungles, beaches, and caves, take a "super sandal" such as Tevas, which provide excellent support and remain comfortable when wet.

Take a walking shoe with a removable insole, choosing a light-weight, open-weave model. For the tropics, avoid leather because it is too heavy and does not dry.

The second pair should be a sturdy, comfortable sandal or walking shoe. For this you could use your Tevas or a supportive sandal such as those made by Clark's. You will wear these every day for traveling and walking. Women may want a lightweight pair of espadrilles or sandals for dress.

Desert Travel

Desert trips are characterized by dry, sunny weather with lots of wind and dust. Desert gear should include a dustbag for your camera, eyedrops such as Visine for dust, Solarcaine if you burn, wide-brimmed cap or hat, one or two large bandanas for dust, spare sunglasses, and, if you wear contacts, extra eyewash, lens cleaner, and glasses or goggles to protect against dust.

If on safari, choose comfortable clothing for long days spent riding in vans. Evening wear for the city and hotel is a bit dressier. Depending on your destination, and time of year, you may need extra layers for warmth. Take the Basic Adventure Wardrobe, with the following changes:

- ▼ 2–4 T-shirts
- ▼ 2 long-sleeved shirts (1 light for sunny days; 1 warmer for cool evenings)
- ▼ 2 pairs of pants, 1 in cotton or cotton/polyester twill; 1 in lighter weight, such as cotton/nylon, cotton/polyester sheeting, or supplex nylon
- ▼ Consider a warm fleece jacket or sweater for cold nights, and a windbreaker

Summer Hiking/Cycling/Hosteling Travel

Bring a super-light wardrobe for a summer of hosteling and hiking or cycling. For cycling, take cotton underwear, three pairs of socks, and substitute sturdy walking or cycling shoes for the hiking boots. If you want to dress up in the city, add one simple nice outfit. Take the Basic Adventure Wardrobe with the following changes.

- ▼ 1 long-sleeved shirt instead of 2
- ▼ 1 all-purpose wool sweater instead of a light cardigan
- ▼ 1 pair of slacks and 2 pairs of shorts (no skirts)
- ▼ Add 1 waterproof rainjacket and pants or poncho
- ▼ Add 2 pairs of wool socks and 2 pairs of sock liners
- ▼ Substitute sturdy, comfortable hiking boots for walking shoes
- ▼ Add light sneakers for wearing around camp

Beach/Resort/Casual Cruise Travel

The main difference here is fabric, style, and the number of swimsuits. Make use of various styles of T-shirts, cotton gauze skirts, polyester crepe de chine and cotton or cotton/blend knits. To the Basic Adventure or Basic Carry-on Wardrobe, adjust as follows:

- ▼ 2 swimsuits instead of 1, plus a pareo or cover-up
- ▼ Add 1 T-shirt dress and/or scoop-neck jumper (for day or evening)
- ▼ Add 1 windbreaker for beach walks
- ▼ Take 2 pairs of sandals, 1 for walking, 1 for evening
- ▼ Take colorful beads, fabric belts, and cotton scarves
- ▼ Add 1 compact outfit for "formal" evenings

▼ Gear for Adventure Travel

- ☐ money pouch or belt for carrying valuables
- ☐ daypack with lock—for carrying cameras and lenses, water bottle, rain gear, and so on. Small pockets are useful for film, sun cream, and sunglasses. Look for padded shoulder straps and waistband. Line the pack with a garbage bag in rainy weather.
- ☐ convertible pack; the zipper should lock. Line the pack with a heavy-gauge garbage bag.
- ☐ expandable nylon totebag—for storing city clothes at the hotel or in a locker while in the field
- ☐ luggage lock and tags
- ☐ personal prescriptions, medications, antibiotics (if necessary)
- ☐ first-aid kit with small booklet, IAMAT doctors list (see Resources)

- [ ] malaria pills if needed; antidiarrheal and headache remedies
- [ ] iodine tablets or water purification equipment (see page 34)
- [ ] water bottle—a wide-mouth bottle is best if you plan to bring drink mixes
- [ ] pocket knife
- [ ] sunglasses and retainer strap (get glasses that offer good UV protection)
- [ ] mosquito repellent; mosquito netting (headnet or other), if desired; mosquito itch-aid
- [ ] sunscreen or sunblock cream with a Sun Protection Factor (SPF) of 15 or higher
- [ ] lip sunblock with an SPF of 15 or higher (such as Chapstick 15, A-fil, or Labiosan)
- [ ] headlamp, Beam-and-Read light, or flashlight—for reading or writing in your journal at night. Take 2 sets of extra batteries and bulbs if you read at night
- [ ] toilet paper—remove the cardboard tube
- [ ] Packtowl or a small, thin towel
- [ ] sewing kit
- [ ] bandana
- [ ] travel alarm or watch with alarm
- [ ] journal, stationery, and pen
- [ ] generous supply of plastic bags to protect your belongings from water—Ziploc bags, plastic garbage bags to line your suitcase, shopping bags, and 1 large bag for dirty laundry
- [ ] toiletries kit: toothbrush and paste, biodegradable shampoo and soap, deodorant, skin moisturizer, nail brush, nail clippers, small packages of Kleenex and Wash'n Dris, razor, shaving cream, baby powder, laundry soap. Adequate supplies of sanitary items.
- [ ] spare eyeglass(es) and spare prescription sunglasses or clip-ons as a back-up; eyeglass straps. Contact lenses can be worn successfully, but be sure to bring a sufficient supply of solutions, including in-the-eye lubricants. An eyeglass repair kit is also handy.

8 | Traveling with Kids

You *can* go carry-on with kids! The strategy is three-fold: Choose luggage and equipment that enhances your mobility; make every person as self-sufficient as possible; and abandon the notion that you take everything with you. A few well-chosen garments, snacks, toys, books, and tapes will be all your family needs to keep going. Your best bet is to buy babies and small children a ticket. This guarantees them a seat and their carry-on luggage allotment. If this is not an option, check with your airlines about their carry-on regulations.

▼ Luggage

Choose a luggage and equipment configuration that will enable you to balance bags and kids as you negotiate airports, planes, and crowds. The convertible backpack/daypack system works best for parents and six-year-old kids and older (between 3 feet, 6 inches and 5 feet, 2 inches tall). Kids can easily carry their own luggage on their backs. Small children, between the ages of three and five, can pack a small duffel or a daypack with their belongings. Make sure it complements your luggage as you may end up carrying it.

Tough Traveler manufactures KidSYSTEMS, a full line of luggage, packs, child-carriers, and daypacks especially for children. Those between the ages of five and eleven can carry the versatile Mini-Van, a frameless convertible pack/suitcase. Held horizontally, it is a single-cavity suitcase. Turn it vertically, open the flap, and out comes a full padded waistband and set of shoulder straps. The Camper is an internal-frame pack that gives more support to the back. This model is excellent for lots of walking and hiking as well as for all-purpose travel. Kids over the age of nine (between 4 feet, 6 inches and 5 feet, 6 inches tall) interested in an internal-frame pack suitable for all trips including extensive hiking will love The Ranger. Children eleven or older will enjoy The Caravan, a larger version of the Mini-Van frameless convertible pack/suitcase with lots of added outside pockets. At this age, depending on their size, kids can also wear adult 22-inch carry-on packs such as The Vagabond made by MEI.

For a trip without a lot of luggage handling, Tough Traveler makes a 17.5-inch cordura nylon Kid's Flight Bag, a suitcase with handles and a shoulder strap that has three compartments for the convenient separation of clean and dirty clothes, and books and toys.

When traveling with babies and small children, parents will find that the convertible pack enables them to travel hands-free to hold the children and a car seat, or to push a stroller. A baby front- or side-carrier can be worn at the same time. Or one parent might wear the child in a backpack type of child carrier and carry a suitcase that has a shoulder strap or tow a wheeled bag. An additional umbrella stroller may be added if you have several small children. If necessary, a sturdy luggage cart such as the Remin Concorde III will carry numerous bags easily.

Take an expandable nylon suitcase that folds up in a small pouch. You will find a hundred purposes for this bag. The best one is that, if your carry-on allotment is limited, you can pack your baby's belongings in your own luggage and then whisk out the tote and transfer baby's gear while settling in for your flight.

All children, including infants, require a passport for foreign travel. Keep passports, money, traveler's checks, and tickets in a security wallet worn underneath your clothing. Two parents can divide multiple passports between them. A parent traveling alone with several children should wear two wallets to store valuables. Include prescription photocopies for medicine (both for you and your child), your child's medical information, and the number of your pediatrician and health insurance plan on your address list. (The checklist on page 29 details the items that should be safeguarded in your security wallet.)

Instead of carrying a big purse, keep a small change purse or a nylon zip bag or wallet in the diaper bag for access to cash. A fanny pack will also work (but do not use it for valuables).

▼ Self-Sufficiency

Make each family member as self-sufficient as possible. This increases a child's sense of participation and lessens the burden on parents. Let kids pack their own daypack with a light jacket or sweatshirt, bottle or cup of juice, snack, and a few favorite books, toys, tapes, and a personal tape player. One parent can keep a backup stock of food in his or her luggage or a soft insulated cooler bag with a shoulder strap. A fanny pack is also useful, especially if the child is already carrying their backpack. Make sure to pack a lightweight daypack in the suitcase, though, for day hikes and excursions.

▼ Food

Hungry children are no fun on the road. Make sure each child is equipped with a water bottle and snacks. Apples, grapes, and other fruit that does not drip or stain, dried fruit, crackers, cereal or bagels, granola bars, trail mix, and cheese-and-cracker packs are good choices. Get kids into the habit of drinking plain water when they are thirsty and you eliminate the constant need to buy or deal with juices that can stain clothes.

Bottle-fed babies should have enough for regular feedings and for two more meals in case you get delayed. Toddlers and small children should have finger foods in sandwich bags. Consider bringing a bag lunch on the flight if your child is a picky eater. Food may not always be available at baby's feeding times and toddlers may not like what is served. (You can request "baby" and "toddler" meals from the airline in advance.) Juice and water are usually available on the flight.

Take-off and landing are good times to give children a bottle, let them nurse, or eat a snack. This will help alleviate possible ear pain caused by changes in air pressure.

▼ Entertainment

Choose items carefully for their portability and value. Simple items that rely on children's creativity, manipulation, and imagination will outlast items that stimulate superficially. I find that books and story cassette tape sets are the best form of entertainment (after Mom and Dad, that is). You can buy and trade books along the way, and have them sent to you during a long trip. Make sure to bring a book with the words to songs, activities, and fingerplay. Below I list several practical and entertaining items for each age group.

Babies

- ▼ 2 or 3 board books (vinyl are especially light)
- ▼ Rattles, especially those with moving parts, or dangling things such as plastic keys or measuring spoons
- ▼ A soft cloth ball
- ▼ Teethers (such as a toothbrush)
- ▼ Nesting objects
- ▼ Mirror (use your pocket mirror)

Toddlers

- ▼ A "Bag of Tricks"—a purse or sandwich bag with odd things they are not normally allowed to play with, or a plastic seven-day medicine dispenser filled with raisins and cereal (the child will be busy for hours opening and closing the caps)
- ▼ Picture books and cassette tapes
- ▼ A book of songs such as *Wee Sing* so a parent can sing to them
- ▼ Finger puppets
- ▼ A favorite doll with a doll-sized blanket
- ▼ Art materials: crayons and paper; a small paintbrush and "Paint with Water" coloring books
- ▼ Duplos

Small Children (Over Three Years Old)

- ▼ Storybooks with cassettes to be used with a Walkman and headphones (my son listened to *Sleeping Beauty* for three straight hours in the car)
- ▼ Art materials: paper and paper bags, string, pipe cleaners, blunt scissors to practice cutting, Scotch tape, crayons, chalk, a paint brush and a "Paint-with-Water" book, dot-to-dot books
- ▼ An erasable travel slate (look for the lighter cardboard type)
- ▼ Portable dolls and play figures
- ▼ Legos

- ▼ A tennis ball
- ▼ Small cars or a small pouch of micro-cars
- ▼ A small divided plastic pill box useful for collecting small things, which kids love to do

Older Children

- ▼ Walkman with tapes and headphones, or microcassette recorder for recording stories, chronicling the trip, and so on
- ▼ Books; a tiny atlas
- ▼ Art materials: paper, scissors, and tape or gluestick, sketch pad, colored pencils, sharpener
- ▼ Journal and pens
- ▼ Small cars
- ▼ Small travel games (magnetic checkers, electronic games, etc.)
- ▼ Cards (get a small book of card games so you can play all kinds)
- ▼ Camera and film
- ▼ Crafts (for example, string and beads for making necklaces, needlepoint, crocheting, and so on)

▼ Clothing

Use the rules for grown-ups when packing for kids.

- ▼ Pack as minimally as possible, taking into account your laundry schedule. Try the "wash-one/wear-one" plus minimal backup strategy. If you wish to launder only once a week, you will need to add clothing.
- ▼ Choose a color scheme for mix and match. All pieces should coordinate. This makes it easier for kids to dress themselves.
- ▼ Pay *extra* attention to layering. Babies and kids are especially at risk in cold weather. Each item of clothing should function as part of a layering system, complete with a moisture-wicking inner layer, insulating layer(s), and an outer layer. Do not forget to protect the extremities with hats, gloves, mittens, balaclavas, and so on.

- Pack separates—they are more versatile and layer easily. They also make diaper changing easier. Add a couple of sleepers for infants.

- Choose easy-care, fast-drying fabrics in various light and medium weights. Denim should be limited to soft lightweight overalls that dry quickly.

- Choose dark colors and prints whenever possible—these conceal stains (this goes for the parents of small kids, too).

Packing Tips

Older kids and teenagers can use the Bundle Method. Put a packing list in their luggage for repacking so that they will not forget anything.

For smaller kids, roll outfits together so they can easily unpack and dress themselves. (If everything is color-coordinated, any choice they make will be presentable.) You can put rubber bands around the bundles or put them in plastic bags, if you like.

Keep the nice outfit (including shoes, socks, and hair accessories) in a plastic bag or stuff sack.

Set aside one play outfit (such as sturdy overalls) for getting really dirty—the rest should then remain relatively clean.

Appoint one person to carry all the swimsuits in a stuff sack, another the pajamas, and so on. This will speed up unpacking.

Clothing for unticketed babies and toddlers may have to go in the parent's suitcase. Lay the clothes neatly on top of the bundle or in one section of your suitcase.

Laundry

Each person can carry their own soiled clothing in a stuff sack. A laundry bag is convenient for car travel. I like the Over-the-Door Neat Net (available at Toys R Us), a large nylon mesh hamper with two hooks that hangs up out of the way. The expandable nylon tote also makes a good hamper.

To prevent stains ban popsicles, powdered drink mixes, and gelatin desserts, which contain dye; mustard; and dark red fruits and fruit juices from your menu. Carry a pretreat spot-and-stain-remover stick along with a flask of water to prevent stains from setting until you can launder them. For a laundry checklist, see pages 38–40.

Layering Strategies for Children

Because of their small size and activity habits, children are more at risk for cold than adults are. Patagonia, a clothing company that makes functional layering pieces for babies, children, and adults, offers this advice.

BABIES AND TODDLERS

Babies have less insulating fat than older children have. They are also fairly sedentary, being carried in a pack or stroller. Dress babies and toddlers up to two years old in warm thin layers with a hat and, because they cannot communicate discomfort verbally, look often for signs of cold or overheating. Feel their extremities—ears, nose, fingers, and toes. Fleece bunting bags are ideal.

THREE- TO SIX-YEAR-OLDS

Little kids may be so busy playing that their sensations go unnoticed. They need a wicking layer and clothing that is easily put on and taken off. Jackets and pants need to have growing room with no loss of insulation.

KIDS OVER SIX

Kids need a wicking layer along with insulation and a shell that they can easily manipulate as temperatures and exertion vary. Do not let a child's enthusiasm exceed its common sense. Children often want to keep on playing rather than come indoors just because they are cold.

OLDER KIDS

Older kids want the function and style of adult gear. They are able to use technical features. They're old enough to understand the potential warning signs and dangers of cold and can easily use a layering system.

PROTECT THE EXTREMITIES

Over half the body heat a child produces can be lost through the head. In cold or wet weather always cover a young child's head and neck with a hat or insulating hood. Protect their faces with scarves, bala-clavas, and neck gaiters in windy weather. Gloves can be worn under mittens. Two pairs of socks add warmth (make sure shoes or boots are sized to accommodate them).

▼ A Child's Travel Wardrobe

This wardrobe will do for children of all ages. Note additions for infants.

MINIMALIST

Layer 1 – Underlayer

- ▼ 3 T-shirts (1 extra-large for pool or beach cover-up)
- ▼ 5–8 sets of underpants
- ▼ 1 pair of tights or leggings
- ▼ 1 swimsuit
- ▼ 1 pair of pajamas—a fleece-type blanket sleeper replaces blankets

For babies add:

- ▼ 1 or 2 sleepers
- ▼ 2 onesies (T-shirts that snap at the crotch)

Layer 2 – Clothing

- ▼ 2 long-sleeved shirts (1 light)
- ▼ 2 or 3 long pants or overalls (1 can be sweatpants if cool weather is expected)
- ▼ 2 pairs of shorts or skirts (or 1 of each)
- ▼ 1 sweatshirt with a hood *or* a thin warm sweater
- ▼ 1 nice outfit, if needed

Layer 3 – Outerlayer

- ▼ Packable rainjacket with hood

Layer 4 – Extremities

- ▼ 5 pairs of socks *or* 2 pairs of infant booties
- ▼ 1 pair of sneakers
- ▼ 1 pair of sandals or thongs
- ▼ 1 pair of dress shoes, if needed

- Sunhat with a wide brim, a means of tying it in wind (chin tie, elasticized headband); ear and neck flaps are good too; such hats are made by Flap Happy.

For cold-weather travel add:

- Silk or polyester knit long underwear top and bottom
- 3 pairs of thin socks for sock liners
- A Polarfleece baby bag, vest, or jacket
- An appropriate outershell
- Glove liners, mittens
- A wool or fleece hat, with ear flaps

Special Accessories for Kids

- I.D. bracelet—This all-important device helps locate lost children. Write or tape the child's name, current hotel, and phone number to the underside. If traveling abroad, indicate "U.S. Embassy" also. (See Resources)
- Packtowl—Packtowls are invaluable for sponging, mopping, wiping, and so on. Buy at least one, cut one-third of it into small washcloths and use the other two-thirds as a towel or mop-up cloth.
- Travel pillow—You can find baby-sized travel pillows at Toys R Us. Inflatable pillows are available from Easy Going and other stores.
- Nightlight—Do not forget one of these for unfamiliar hotel rooms. You need a converter and adapter for foreign destinations.
- Hamper—Over-the-Door Neat Net is a mesh laundry bag perfect for fixed-base trips because it hangs up out of the way and is very lightweight. Available at Toys R Us.

▼ Equipment for Babies and Small Children

To go carry-on you can take at most a car seat and/or (depending on the airline) a portable umbrella stroller or a child-carrier onto the plane. Arrange, rent, or borrow cribs and other equipment in advance.

Car Seat

If you will be driving, you will need an FAA-approved car seat. This will also provide a comfortable place for the baby to eat and sleep. Some car rental agencies rent car seats, too. A revolutionary alternative for babies that weigh over 25 pounds is the FAA-approved Travel Vest by AOK, a packable 5-point harness that may be attached to a car or airline seat belt. (See Lullaby Lane in Resources.)

If the flight is not full (call ahead), it pays to bring the car seat with you to the gate. If there is room, they will seat you next to an empty seat; if the plane is full, the crew will stow or check the car seat. You can always ask them to keep it inside the cabin; they may oblige.

Umbrella Stroller

If you will be driving and your sightseeing stops are accessible to strollers (some museums do not allow them), take a compact umbrella stroller with small, sturdy, easily maneuvered double wheels that collapses easily and can be carried with one hand.

Backpack Child Carriers

Carrying a child on your back is ideal if you will be taking public transportation, hiking, or walking on terrain where strollers are not convenient. Backpack carriers also provide freer access for the parent maneuvering in crowds, stores, and other public places. A small child can remain in a backpack carrier all day, resting, sightseeing, and sleeping at will. Tough Traveler manufactures frame child carriers for kids between the ages of six months (when they can sit with their heads unsupported) and four years. These carriers collapse and are easily stowed in the overhead bin. Gerry Products also makes a good line of child carriers.

When choosing a child carrier, consider its primary use and your comfort and well as baby's. If the pack will be baby's sole mode of transportation with lots of all day hiking and walking (and baby sleeping), Tough Traveler's highly technical Kid Carrier will be most comfortable for parent and child. It takes loads of up to 50 pounds and fits parents between 5 feet, 1 inch and 6 feet, 4 inches tall. The carrier has fully padded straps and waistbands, back ventilation, and lots of control straps to distribute the load. The even more elaborate Stallion assures long-range comfort (all day and longer hiking) when carrying loads of up to 60 pounds. This one is appropriate for giving older children a respite. For a simpler, less expensive pack ideal for local trips and short hikes, The Montana still offers parents control straps and a sternum (chest) strap to fine-tune the load.

All packs have a large pouch under the seat for storing diapers, gear, and snacks. Optional equipment includes a rain or sun hood, stirrups, and on the Kid Carrier, a side pocket set.

Take a small pocket mirror along so that you can see your child, and make sure she's wearing her hat.

Soft Carriers for Infants

Soft infant carriers are convenient for holding infants between birth and nine months of age on the parent's body in a hands-free mode. Easily stowed, they are ideal for travel. Tummy packs such as those made by Gerry, Tough Traveler, and many other companies, handle babies up to nine months of age. Choose one that supports the baby's head and allows baby to see out. A quick-drying fabric is an advantage. Sara's Ride is a soft carrier designed for infants able to sit up; the child rides sitting on the parent's hip.

Harnesses

Harnesses are quite helpful for keeping tabs on wandering toddlers in crowded airports and train stations when you have a great deal of luggage. Harnesses also eliminate the need for a playpen. Be careful not to let the child get tangled up.

A Place to Sleep

Portable cribs have no place as carry-on luggage; consider other sleeping arrangements.

For babies that cannot crawl yet:

▼ Use your blanket to line a drawer for baby to sleep in.

▼ Baby Bjorn makes an inflatable changing cushion with sides; this will do for a baby who cannot climb out.

▼ Make a small bed-roll: Cut a piece of insulite bought from a camping store and cover it with a large rubberized protector pad and a small sheet. Roll everything up and strap it to the bottom of your travel pack.

For crawlers and toddlers:

▼ Pack a small inflatable pool that you can lay on the floor and line with a blanket or pad.

▼ Right Start Catalog (800) 548-8531 offers a travel bed that rolls up. It weighs three pounds and measures 40 inches long by 25 inches wide.

▼ Transfer the child onto a child-sized sleeping pad (such as EVA blue foam or Therm-a-Rest, that you carry strapped to your luggage) after the child has fallen asleep on your bed.

▼ Push a bed against the wall and flank it with chairs to make sure the child cannot roll off.

Diapers

If you will be traveling where baby supplies are available, pack light. Bring enough trim extra-absorbent diapers to get you to your destination. Be open minded about other brands if you cannot find the one you know. If you are going off the beaten path, take cloth diapers and wraps that you can wash and reuse as you go (read *Adventuring with Children* by Nan Jeffrey, Foghorn Press, 1992, for more on using cloth diapers). Pack a few extra diapers for emergencies.

▼ Packing Tips

I like to pack kits for kids—a diaper kit, a medical kit, a food kit. Invest in durable, zippered, nylon pouches. An insulated, foldable six-pack bag with a shoulder strap is also handy.

The Diaper/Flight Bag

Let's assume you are allowed one bag for baby and/or toddler. The best investment is the Deluxe Diaper Bag (measuring 16 by 9 by 11 inches; $45) made by Land's End (see Resources). This sturdy high-capacity bag accommodates diapers, wipes, several changes of clothes, books and toys, four bottles or cups in insulated pockets, and between four and eight jars of baby food. It comes with a zippered foldable pouch for baby's toiletries (I use this to make the diaper kit), a removable zippered pouch for wet and soiled items, a compact changing pad, and a front pocket for parent's stuff.

Any large daypack or tote will also serve this purpose, especially if you also have an insulated six-pack, lunch, or bottle bag for bottles and food. The diaper/flight bag should contain:

A DIAPER KIT

A diaper kit is incredibly handy. It can be passed back and forth between parents. After changing baby, restock the bag immediately for your next use. Use any easily identifiable zippered nylon pouch measuring about 7 by 12 inches.

The kit itself consists of 1 diaper, 1 pack of wipes (a travel-sized package or a Ziploc bag filled with wet wipes), 1 rubberized lap pad, 1 compact vinyl changing pad, 1 small tube of diaper rash cream, 2 plastic bags for the soiled diapers.

EXTRA DIAPERS

The remainder of your diaper supply (enough for the first leg of your trip) should be distributed in your suitcases, tucked into corners, or lining edges. You can also use your expandable nylon tote for diapers, and stow it away as they are used up.

▼ Resealable plastic bags in quart and gallon sizes, or a roll of sandwich bags

▼ Baby wipes—Take them out of the original container and place them in a resealable plastic bag.

▼ 2 wet Packtowl washcloths in separate resealable plastic bag—1 for washing hands and faces, 1 as a mop-up cloth for tables, chairs, and so on

▼ Nursing pads

If needed:

▼ 2 all-purpose burp or nursing cover-up cloths—Use thin gauze-type cloth diapers or Packtowl or thin flannel receiving blanket (these dry fast).

▾ Waterproof dropcloth—Disposable Lammies or a 1-yard-square piece of vinyl to be used for protecting beds, too

▾ Toiletry kit—Small bottles of liquid baby soap, which doubles as soap and shampoo, powder if used, baby sunscreen, toothbrush, and baby nail clipper

▾ Pretreat stain and soil remover—Along with cold water, this is good for preventing stains from setting on washables.

Comfort objects

▾ Pacifier, favorite toy, blanket

▾ Toys and books, a few old, a few new

▾ Safety outlet plugs

▾ All-purpose blanket—One compact blanket for baby to play or sleep on, or for use as a nursing cover-up. This can also be a tablecloth for picnics or to create a play area for all kids. I use a thinly quilted cotton/polyester quilt.

Clothing

▾ 2 outfits, including one for arrival. Pack comfortable, nonbinding separates. Include booties if baby is barefoot.

▾ 1 lightweight sweatshirt or nylon jacket with hood

▾ Sunhat

Food

This can be consolidated in the diaper bag or carried separately in an insulated cooler bag.

▾ Finger food—dry cereal, crackers, bagels for baby and older children; cheese-and-cracker packs, fruit leather, raisins for older children

▾ Baby food—dehydrated, 3-ounce jars, or ready-to-serve microwave meals for babies older than 5 months

▾ A small plastic bowl with lid

▾ Spoons—2 sturdy plastic spoons (put long feeding spoons in a toothbrush container)

▾ Bib—laminated or pack of disposables (Lammies)

- ▼ Bottles—one for juice or water and one for formula, or take disposable liners; nipples, rings and caps (1st Years makes a nipple adapter so that you can fit any nipple on disposable-liner bottles)
- ▼ Formula—ready-to-feed and dry, in a Ziploc bag. One method is to fill a 1-cup plastic container with powder and scoop. Keep the container and a bottle filled with water in the food bag to mix when needed. Replenish after use. Maya makes a premeasured 3-feedings cup. Use a pack that you preheat and wrap around the bottle to keep fluids warm.
- ▼ A spill-proof travel cup (if appropriate)

MEDICAL KIT

Add the following items to your own first-aid kit (see page 35) or put them in a place where baby cannot get to them.

- ☐ phone number of your pediatrician, and IAMAT phone number (see Resources)
- ☐ prescription medications and vitamins for baby (try to get those that do not need refrigeration)
- ☐ syrup of Ipecac for accidental poisoning (administer only with medical advice)
- ☐ medicine dispenser
- ☐ thermometer (preferably nonmercury type for air trips)
- ☐ baby acetaminophen
- ☐ antidiarrheal medication (ask your doctor)
- ☐ children's decongestant
- ☐ insect repellent (low-dose DEET for kids) and an anti-sting or itch treatment, such as calamine lotion, Benadryl, and so on

9 | Packing for Teens

Why a separate chapter for teenagers? There are two reasons. One, teens are very fashion-conscious and tend to overpack. Two, they underestimate the necessity to protect their valuables.

Experienced teen travelers know that traveling light is the way to go. Forget that big suitcase! Get a convertible backpack with a detachable daypack (see page 12), use the Bundle Method outlined in chapter 5, and you will be set to go to camp, Europe, or any study program for weeks or months.

If you love fashion, here is your challenge: Create the greatest number of outfits possible from the fewest pieces of clothing, using layering principles along the way. Start early and refine your wardrobe before the trip. Then pack it and walk a mile. If you cannot handle it easily, go home and start throwing items out.

Follow the wardrobe guidelines outlined in earlier chapters. Here are the key points:

If traveling abroad, choose clothing that is appropriate, in terms of culture and climate, for your destination. Ask your sponsoring hosts or others who have been there. Shorts, revealing clothing, and sports clothing, for example, are not acceptable in many locales. Skirts may be more appropriate than slacks would be. One-piece swimsuits may be more acceptable than bikinis. If you are visiting religious sites take a scarf to cover your head and shoulders.

Coordinate your clothing around a two-color scheme. Add a third or fourth color for accents. If all your items are interchangeable, you can create a wide variety of outfits. Separates will add flexibility. Choose loose, comfortable clothing that will accommodate a security wallet.

If you are handwashing, leave your jeans home. They are hard to wash by hand and dry very slowly.

All items of clothing should function as part of a layering system. Instead of a few bulky items, pack several thin layers, including insulating underwear, short- and long-sleeved shirts, a sweater, and outergear.

Use accessories to add variety. Colorful belts, hair decorations, hose, and socks do not weigh much. Unless you are traveling where none will be available, take only what makeup and toiletries you need and whatever you can decant into small plastic bottles or use sample sizes. Remember that you have only two clothing colors so you do not need much makeup. If you will be gone a long time, have mom or dad ship you some of your favorite shampoo midway through your trip.

The following wardrobe list is based on the one recommended by the Council on International Educational Exchange (CIEE) in its excellent and highly recommended book *Going Places: The High School Student's Guide to Study, Travel, and Adventure Abroad* (St. Martin's Press). Refer also to the Basic Adventure Wardrobe lists in chapter 7. This wardrobe will fit into a convertible pack and suffice for short or long spring and summer trips. Remember, the less you pack the more room you have for things you buy!

▼ Travel Wardrobe for Teens

For short trips pack the minimum number of items recommended. Adjust the mixture of slacks, skirts, and shorts depending on your personal style, the cultural customs of your destination, and your planned activities. Choose light and medium weights in easy-care fabrics. Pack a sweater in an accessible place.

Clothes

In your main bag, pack:

Layer 1 – Underlayer

- ▼ 2 T-shirts to go with skirts as well as pants (for boys, polo-type are more versatile)
- ▼ 1 extra-large T-shirt (beach cover-up, nightshirt)
- ▼ 1 pair of leggings or tights for extra warmth or sleeping
- ▼ 4–7 pairs of underpants
- ▼ 7 pairs of socks
- ▼ 4–5 pairs of hose or tights, if needed (more if you wear an odd size)
- ▼ 2 or 3 bras

▼ 1 bathing suit

Layer 2 – Clothing

▼ 2 pairs of long pants

▼ 1 or 2 skirts

▼ 1 short-sleeved blouse or shirt

▼ 1 or 2 long-sleeved shirts (1 light for sun protection, 1 heavier)

▼ 1 pair of shorts (knee-length)

▼ 1 or 2 sweaters or jackets (1 nice, *thin* warm sweater, and 1 sweatshirt or a casual jacket)

▼ 1 dressy outfit in packable fabric, if needed

▼ Sport clothing as needed

Layer 3 – Outerlayer

▼ 1 rainjacket with hood

▼ 1 travel umbrella if needed

Layer 4 – Extremities

▼ 1 pair of sneakers or walking shoes

▼ 1 pair of sandals or thongs

▼ 1 pair of dress shoes

▼ 1 or 2 belts

▼ 1 small, packable purse

▼ Bandanas, scarves

▼ Cap or packable sunhat

▼ Tie, hair accessories, jewelry (not valuable)

Gear for Teens

Also in your main bag pack the following, not all of which you may need (see chapter 3 for details):

▼ Toiletry kit (with small and sample-sized containers)

▼ Small dual-voltage travel steamer, iron, or hairdryer with appropriate adapter plugs (try to avoid this sort of equipment)

▼ Towel (a Packtowl or half a thin terry towel and a baby washcloth)

- ▼ Some resealable plastic bags (sandwich and gallon size)
- ▼ Travel alarm clock
- ▼ Flashlight and extra batteries
- ▼ First-aid kit
- ▼ Sewing kit
- ▼ Laundry kit
- ▼ Eating utensils (cup, spoon, fork, plastic plate)
- ▼ Pictures of your family and home to show new friends
- ▼ Guidebooks and maps, or photocopied pages in manila envelopes
- ▼ Fold-up, expandable, nylon totebag
- ▼ Inflatable pillow and ear plugs for noisy hotels
- ▼ Small gifts for your hosts

In your daypack or totebag pack:

- ▼ Eyeglasses and sunglasses
- ▼ Sunscreen, lip balm
- ▼ Cosmetic kit (keep it small!)
- ▼ Water bottle
- ▼ Pocket knife
- ▼ Journal or diary, pens, postcards, stationery
- ▼ Small camera and film
- ▼ Personal tape player, tapes, headphones
- ▼ Book, games, cards
- ▼ Current map, guidebook, brochures
- ▼ Snack

▼ Security for Teens

Some teens think of a money belt as an unnecessary hassle that will spoil their outfits. They also feel immune from theft of important items such as a passport, their traveler's checks, cash, credit cards, phone card, airline tickets, student I.D., and so on.

Chances are, nothing will happen. But do not tempt people who are in the business of stealing from unsuspecting travelers. You do not need to be paranoid; just be smart and take responsibility for your personal and material security. Keep your valuables in a money pouch and wear it *at all times* when you are traveling around, sleeping on the train, or staying in a hostel. Do not leave anything valuable in your luggage or daypack. Wear the pouch hidden *under your clothing*, not hanging around your neck outside your shirt—this is an open invitation to thieves. (I do not even like the neck strap to show under my shirt.)

Luckily, hassle-free security wallets are comfortable and their contents accessible. The best choice is Eagle Creek's Undercover Security Wallet. This vertical pouch has an adjustable strap that you can wear in a variety of ways. The best way to wear it is around your waist, tucked down inside your slacks, skirt, or shorts like a hanging pocket. It is easy to pull in and out, and you don't have to wear a belt. If you are wearing tight pants or a skirt (clothes are more comfortable when they are loose-fitting, by the way), the wallet can also be worn around the neck under your shirt (do not let the neck straps show). Or you can shorten the cord and wear the pouch underneath your arm like a holster, or lengthen it and wear it diagonally across your chest, with the pouch tucked into your pants or skirt.

The pouch has three pockets: one long, zippered compartment for traveler's checks, tickets, documents, cash, and so on; an open pocket for your passport and passes, and a third, small zippered pocket on the flap for credit cards and a bit of cash and change. I really like this small pocket: when the pouch is tucked in, you can lift out the flap to have quick access to tip money without having to pull out the whole wallet. For more on security, see the following chapter.

If you develop the skill of packing right and protecting yourself now, you will be prepared to become a real *traveler,* not just a tourist—mobile enough to wander the world, meet wonderful people, and see wonderful places.

10 Security

As a carry-on traveler, you avoid the risk of lost and pilfered luggage. Here are some other precautions you can take to protect yourself and your belongings. For a complete discussion of security and contingency planning, read *The Safe Travel Book* by Peter Savage (Macmillan, 1993). Many of the tips mentioned below come from his book.

▼ Protecting Travel Documents and Valuables

Wear a security wallet *at all times*, whether you are awake or asleep, and hide any visible straps. The best model is the adjustable World Class Passport Carrier by Coconuts, which has a steel cable running through the straps so that it cannot be cut off. Many other types are available. See pages 26–29 for a full discussion.

Always carry your passport, cash, half of your traveler's checks, your credit cards, address and phone list, and copies of prescriptions in that security wallet. Do not be tempted to pack them anywhere else. To split your risk, carry the remaining half of your traveler's checks in your luggage. Pack your traveler's check record separately from your checks.

Give a home contact copies of all your documents, including your passport, credit card account numbers, redemption center phone numbers, and itinerary. This person can cancel your credit cards if they are lost or stolen, and send you copies overnight of anything you need quickly.

You may store valuables in the hotel safe deposit box if you feel that the hotel security is untrustworthy. Make sure the safe's contents are covered by the hotel's insurance coverage. Get a signed, itemized receipt for the items stored.

If you must store valuables in your room, hide them. You can buy hide-a-safes of various sorts, or make a safe by cutting the inner pages out of a paperback book. But the best strategy of all is to travel without valuables.

At the beach, put your valuables in a Seal Pack or other water-tight security wallet (see page 28) that you can wear while swimming.

As much as possible, use traveler's checks and credit cards instead of cash.

For incidental expenses, carry only a little cash in local currency or small U.S. bills in your luggage, front pocket, fanny pack, or wallet in a front pocket or an inside jacket pocket. *Everything* else should be in your security wallet at all times.

Do not put valuables in a purse and, if someone tugs at your purse, let it go.

Do not wear expensive looking jewelry and watches. They attract attention.

Include the following phone numbers on your address list, carried in your security wallet:

▼ Your contact person at home who has copies of all documents

▼ The U.S. embassy and the 24-hour telephone number of the U.S. mission. These numbers are available from the State Department in Washington, D.C., (202) 647-4000.

▼ Numbers for reporting lost or stolen credit cards and traveler's check centers (including any after-hours number)

▼ Your travel agent's 24-hour number, if any

▼ Your emergency medical insurance company's 24-hour assistance number or the number of an English-speaking doctor (see IAMAT under Resources)

▼ Your automobile insurance company's emergency assistance number

▼ Your long-distance calling-card assistance number as well as any additional country codes you may need. When using the telephone, memorize your card code and shield your fingers when inputting your card number (a common scam is for thieves at airports to steal your card number by watching you punch your number in), or use phones that allow you to slide the card through.

Leave important items that you are unlikely to need while traveling, such as social security and local credit cards, at home.

▼ Luggage

Do not use expensive-looking luggage. It attracts attention. Label each piece of luggage inside and out with your name and *business* address or your next destination. Be sure your luggage is locked. If you check luggage through, watch to make sure it is tagged and routed properly. Attach a luggage strap, colored yarn, or tape to help you identify your bag when you retrieve it.

At the airport, thieves steal bags off the X-ray machine's conveyor belt while the owner is walking through the metal detector. Make sure that you can go through the detector quickly by putting all metal items, such as large belt buckles, keys, and anything else that might set off the metal detector, inside your carry-on *in advance*. Then, after putting your luggage on the conveyor, do not take your eyes off it. If you are traveling with a companion take turns going through the detector and watching your luggage.

While waiting, keep your luggage between your ankles. Consider using a retractable cable lock (made by Eagle Creek) to fasten luggage to a bench or fence if you will be waiting long.

Keep any valuables, such as a camera, binoculars, and so on, locked in your daypack or totebag.

If you want to take a short day trip, check your luggage and equipment at the train station.

In many places, daypacks and purses are commonly slashed and items are stolen without your even noticing. To prevent losing your belongings, you can line the sides and bottom of your bag or fanny pack with gutter screen to be found at the hardware store.

▼ Medicine

Carry half your medicine with you in your daypack, the other half in your main bag. Carry prescription copies in your security wallet.

▼ Personal Security

IN YOUR HOTEL

▼ Maintain heightened awareness at all times; this is your best protection.

- ▼ Be alert when checking in and out of a hotel; do not flash your cash around.
- ▼ Learn the location of hotel exits.
- ▼ Book a room near a busy area or an elevator.
- ▼ Make sure your room has a peephole and double dead bolts. You can pack a portable lock (see Resources).
- ▼ Call the front desk to verify unexpected deliveries.
- ▼ Small hotels are generally safer than large facilities. Strangers are instantly noticed.
- ▼ Small intruder alarms and smoke alarms are available. Consider these.

AROUND TOWN

- ▼ Do not look vulnerable or lost. Walk with a purpose and stay alert to what's happening around you.
- ▼ Ask the hotel about the safety of a neighborhood and about areas to be avoided. Ask whether it is safe to walk alone.
- ▼ Ask the concierge for directions and costs before taking a cab.
- ▼ Conventioneers: If you are attending a convention, obtain advance information about the city (maps and guides will be your best sources) and, when there, remove your name tag when your are out of the convention area.

IN YOUR RENTAL CAR

- ▼ Have keys in hand when you approach the car. Look in, around, and under the car before getting in.
- ▼ Plan your route before you leave. Tourists stopped at a traffic light and looking at a map are targets for theft and carjackings.
- ▼ Keep your car in gear when stopped at a light.
- ▼ Ask directions from officials.

Remember—most trips are uneventful. Just exercise the same precautions that you do at home, and you are bound to have a safe and enjoyable trip.

A1 The Top Ten Packing Tips for Carry-on Travelers

1. Buy the right luggage.

2. Make a packing list *at least* a week ahead of time (thinking of the weather and activities on your trip), so you can focus on your needs and have time to shop.

3. Choose a color scheme for your clothing and stick to it.

4. For clothes, pack simply styled separates in maintainable fabrics.

5. Pack small sizes of toiletries. Remove all excess packaging.

6. When in doubt, leave it out!

7. Before your trip, pack your bag and walk a quarter mile with it. If you can't manage it, take out extras.

8. Wear valuables in a security wallet only, even for short trips.

9. Mail home souvenirs, purchases, etc. as you travel, so they don't weigh you down.

10. Don't forget the most important things to make your trip enjoyable: your flexibility and sense of humor!

A2 Resources

Luggage and Accessories

Easy Going Travel Shop and Bookstore
Mail orders: (800) 675-5500
FAX: (510) 843-4152

1385 Shattuck Avenue
Berkeley, CA 94709
(510) 843-3533

1617 Locust Street
Walnut Creek, CA 94569
(510) 947-6660

Many of the items mentioned in this book are available at Easy Going Travel Shop and Bookstore in Berkeley and Walnut Creek, California. Among many other things, they sell carry-on luggage (Easy Going Special Edition Bag, Club USA, Florentine, Travelpro Rollaboard, MEI travel packs); organizing aids (including core pouches such as Carry-Rite Mini-Organizers and Judy Gilford's Deluxe Core Pouch), zippered nylon pouches, expandable totebags and daypacks, and security wallets (Coconuts' World Class Passport Carrier, Eagle Creek Undercover Security Wallet, Seal Pack, and others); Flexo-line, Packtowls, Remin luggage carts, electrical travel appliances, converters and adapters, travel soap and spot removers, water-purification devices, and rainwear. They also have a huge selection of travel books and maps. They welcome phone inquiries and mail orders.

Large Transformers and 220V Appliances

Aris Export Company
1501 Vermont Street
San Francisco, CA 94107
(415) 550-8605

This company specializes in 220V appliances and large transformers. They also carry foreign phone jack adapters. No catalog, but they welcome phone inquiries.

Travel Clothing

The following catalogs offer high-quality clothing appropriate for travel. Where noted, other gear and children's clothing are available, too.

Norm Thompson's "Departures" Catalog
(800) 547-1160

This company, which also has three retail stores in Portland, Oregon, has a motto, "Escape from the Ordinary," that describes the merchandise perfectly. Norm Thompson has an unusual selection of versatile, easy-care, classic casual styles for men and women, including the multipocketed Frequent Flyer Travel Jacket, and comfortable shoes. Recommended if you travel on business or want a more tailored look.

Eddie Bauer
(800) 426-6253

Nice selection of high-quality clothing. Silk underwear is also available seasonally.

Land's End
(800) 356-4444

Wide selection of high-quality, simply styled, durable, casual separates and comfortable shoes. Silk and polyester-knit long underwear is available seasonally. Lots for kids, too. Also their own line of soft luggage.

L. L. Bean
(800) 221-4221

All types of high-quality casual separates and outerwear including some microfiber clothing, comfortable shoes, outdoor gear, and luggage. Silk and polyester thermal underwear is available seasonally.

Patagonia and Patagonia Kids
(800) 638-6464

This catalog offers high-performance, functional and attractive clothing for specific climates and activities. Especially interesting is their "A/C" (for air-conditioned) clothing for tropical weather, modest length Baggies long shorts, Synchilla polarfleece clothing, and Capilene polyester-knit thermal underwear. Fascinating is a fleece jacket made from recycled soda bottles. Patagonia also offers its own line of luggage.

The Primary Layer
(800) 282-8206

A nice selection of all types of easy-care underwear including a half slip with hidden pockets for passport and money, nylon boxer shorts and briefs for men, nightwear, socks, and so on.

REI (Recreational Equipment Inc.)
(800) 426-4840 TDD: (800) 443-1988

Catalog and multiple retail locations. This excellent retailer offers all kinds of high-performance outdoor equipment, children's packs and carriers, travel packs, clothing, long underwear, shoes, small eating utensils, and other gear. Check out the convertible slacks—long pants that zip off at the knee to become walking shorts.

TravelSmith Outfitting Guide and Catalog
(800) 950-1600

TravelSmith has done the shopping for you, selecting each garment for its specific travel function as well as attractiveness and durability.

The Walk Shop
2120 Vine Street
Berkeley, CA 94709
(510) 849-3628

Excellent selection of comfortable shoes.

Westwind
715 Santa Cruz Avenue
Menlo Park, CA 94125
(415) 329-8876

300 West Portal Avenue
San Francisco, CA 94127
(415) 664-2671

This unusual retail women's shop sells packable coordinated separates arranged by neutral color scheme and group. The styles are simple and classic, and make perfect travel wardrobes. Accessories, belts, and scarves complete the outfits. A one-stop source for a travel wardrobe. Unfortunately, there is no catalog.

Wintersilks Catalog
(800) 648-7455

Huge selection of silk undergarments, thermal underwear, and clothing for men and women, all available year-round.

Children's Gear

The following sell clothing and other products for children. Also check Toys R Us for many kid's items.

Tough Traveler
1012 State Street
Schenectady, NY 12307
(800) 468-6844

Children's luggage and child carriers are this company's speciality. Tough Traveler products are sold through mail order and outdoor retailers such as REI.

Lullaby Lane
(415) 588-7644

A wide selection of items appropriate for traveling with kids, including the five-point packable safety seatbelt and children's luggage.

Practical Parenting
Dept. ID
Deephaven, MN 55391

Disposable self-closing plastic "I.D. Me" bracelets have a place for the child's name, hotel, and so on, to be written on the underside. For two bracelets, send $1 and a long self-addressed stamped envelope with the appropriate information.

Medic Alert Foundation
(800) 344-3226

Another type of bracelet is the Medic Alert bracelet. Call the Medic Alert Foundation or your drugstore for an order form. The bracelet costs $35.

Books

These are books that I have found to be wonderful resources. Available at bookstores and travel stores.

- ▼ *International Traveler's Weather Guide*, **Tom Loffman and Randy Mann (Weather Press, 1991).** A small paperback with complete weather information and descriptions of every destination—a great tool for planning your wardrobe and accessory needs. It is obtainable from Weather Press, P.O. Box 660606, Sacramento, CA 95866.

- ▼ *Overcoming Jet Lag*, **Dr. Charles F. Ehret and Lynne Waller Scanlon (Berkeley Books, 1983).** All you need to know to minimize the effects of jet lag.

- ▼ *The Pocket Doctor*, **Stephen Bezruchka, M.D. (Mountaineers, 1992).** This book is a handy, pocket-sized take-along guide that covers first-aid and the treatment of a variety of illnesses, bites, infections, and other problems you may encounter on the road.

- ▼ *The Safe Travel Book*, **Peter Savage (Macmillan, 1993).** With all contingencies considered, this is an amazing resource that helps you plan a truly safe trip.

- ▼ *Staying Healthy in Asia, Africa and Latin America*, **Dirk Schroeder (Moon Publications, 1993).** This comprehensive handbook explains medical and health procedures when traveling in developing countries.

Medical Assistance

IAMAT (International Association for Medical Assistance to Travelers)
736 Center Street
Lewiston, NY 14092
(716) 754-4883

IAMAT will give you the names of English-speaking physicians and the locations of hospitals around the world, as well as climate, immunization, and sanitation information.

A3 Questions and Answers

Here are answers to the questions that I get asked most frequently during my packing classes:

What is the best fabric for travel?

Natural fibers, such as pure cotton and wool, breathe the best, but synthetics, such as polyester, lend wrinkle- and stain-resistance and dry faster. Wool and wool/blend gabardine are superior for fall, winter, and spring. Cotton and cotton/blend knits are perfect for spring and summer. (See the fabric chart on page 62 for recommended travel fabrics.)

How many garments can you fit in a suitcase?

Almost every person can pack a basic travel wardrobe (between seven and nine pieces) in a carry-on. How much more you can get in will depend on your size and the length and bulk of your garments. Generally, smaller people will be able to pack between ten and sixteen pieces; larger people possibly no more than the minimum seven or eight. Your jacket is the bulkiest item. If you do not pack that, you will have more room for other clothing.

Does this packing system work for larger shoe and clothing sizes?

The beauty of the Bundle Method (see chapter 5) is that everyone can use it. The number of items of clothing you can fit may, however, be limited by your size. People with larger shoes will need to consolidate as much as possible. If both shoes cannot fit along the bottom edge of the bag, you will need to sacrifice other space. The best strategies are to wear one pair and pack one pair or to take a second bag.

What is the rule of thumb about underwear and socks?

It depends on how much you want to wash. To travel extremely light, take two sets and wash one and wear one. Take eight sets if you want to wash once a week. I generally take four or five sets of each. Take an extra set in cold weather, because things dry more slowly then.

What about galoshes?

Galoshes are great if you are going to very wet weather. They seem to be difficult to find these days, but if you can find a lightweight pair buy it.

How long does it take you to pack?

The hard part of packing is selecting the clothing. Once you have your wardrobe, you will pack clothing in five minutes or less. Repacking accessories takes longer than repacking the clothes.

I tried the Bundle Method and things still got wrinkled. What am I doing wrong?

Two things could have happened. First, the fabrics you chose may not have traveled well. Second, you may not have packed tightly enough. For the Bundle Method to work, the core and inner items must provide sufficient cushioning and the outer layers must be wrapped tightly around the core. If they are loose or underpacked more wrinkling will occur.

Do you use plastic bags or tissue paper?

I do not use any extra packing material. Plastic causes items to shift in the bag, traps heat and moisture in hot weather, and except for garment bags, is difficult to work with. Tissue paper is unnecessary with the Bundle Method. The only extra material I might use is interfacing material to make a partition in the bag between accessories and the bundle.

Do you pack hangers?

I generally pack one small plastic or metal skirt hanger. It goes in my accessory section. I do not use hangers for packing the clothes.

If you are going to be in a different place every day would you still use the Bundle Method?

Yes! Of course, it is a bit different from being able to reach in and pull out one folded garment. The trade-off is you will have less creasing and spend less time ironing. Do not forget, with your efficient travel wardrobe, you will only be working with five to seven packed garments. You will get really quick at folding and unfolding the bundle.

Aren't luggage carts a hassle?

This depends entirely on your situation. The lack of a luggage cart is a hassle if you have more than one bag. Carts are also versatile: They offer wider wheels and step sliders for added stability and you can use them with any bag you already own. They do require that you stop and unload and collapse them before boarding the plane, and they must be stored separately. If you need only one carry-on and are planning to buy a bag, wheeled luggage, such as the Rollaboard by Travelpro, will eliminate the need for an extra piece.

Does the steel cable in the World Class Passport Carrier by Coconuts set off the metal detector at the airport?

No, I have never heard of that happening.

What length of knife blade is allowed on an airplane?

The blade must be no more than 4 inches long to be allowed on the airplane. This goes for scissors too. Pack your knife in your carry-on. If it is in your pocket it may be confiscated until the end of the flight.

What do you do if U.S. customs wants to inspect your belongings?

To decrease the time it takes to repack in case customs asks you to undo your bundle, use the Quick-Fix Method before coming home: Lay all your garments in the bag, stacking the collars in one direction. Drape the sleeves out. Drape the bottoms out. Put in your core. To close the bundle, bring all the left sleeves in, then all the right sleeves. Then the bottoms. Voila! There is your bundle. It is easy to unfurl and to close up again if you get stopped at customs. Remember, don't tempt customs. Have all your paperwork and declarable items ready and waiting to be inspected.

Bibliography

Allen, Jeanne. *Showing Your Colors: A Designer's Guide to Coordinating Your Wardrobe* (Chronicle Books, 1986).

Angelucci, Diane Donofrio. "Washday Stain-Removal Chart," *Baby Talk*, August 1993.

Aslett, Don. *Don Aslett's Stain Buster's Bible: The Complete Guide to Stain Removal* (Plume, 1990).

Axtell, Roger E. *Do's and Taboos Around the World*, 3rd ed. (Wiley, 1993).

Brown, George Albert. *The Airline Passenger's Guerilla Handbook: Strategies and Tactics for Beating the Air Travel System* (Blakes Publishing Group, 1989).

Butler, Arlene Kay. *Traveling with Children and Enjoying It: A Complete Guide to Family Travel by Car, Plane, and Train* (Globe Pequot, 1991).

"Carry-on Luggage," *Consumer Reports*, Oct. 1987.

Cass, Lee Hogan, and Karen E. Anderson. *Look Like a Winner: Why, When, and Where to Wear What* (Putnam, 1985).

Consumer Report Books editors, with Monte Florman and Marjorie Florman, *How to Clean Practically Anything* (Consumer Report Books, 1992).

Council on International Educational Exchange. *Going Places: The High-School Student's Guide to Study, Travel and Adventure* (St. Martin's Press, 1993).

Evatt, Cris. *How to Pack Your Suitcase...and Other Travel Tips* (Fawcett Columbine, 1987).

Feldon, Leah. *Traveling Light: Every Woman's Guide to Getting There in Style* (Putnam, 1985).

Harriman, Cynthia W. *Take Your Kids to Europe* (Mason-Grant, 1991).

Hatt, John. *The Tropical Traveller: An Essential Guide to Travel in Hot Climates* (Hippocrene, 1984).

Jeffrey, Nan, with Kevin Jeffrey. *Adventuring with Children: The Family Pack-Along Guide to the Outdoors and the World* (Foghorn Press, 1992).

Koltun, Frances. *Complete Book for the Intelligent Woman Traveler* (Simon and Schuster, 1967).

Lansky, Vicki. *Trouble-Free Travel with Children: Helpful Hints for Parents on the Go* (The Book Peddlers, 1991).

Loffman, Tom, and Randy Mann. *International Traveler's Weather Guide* (Weather Press, 1991).

REI (Recreational Equipment, Inc.), *FYI* series of consumer information pamphlets.

Savage, Peter. *The Safe Travel Book* rev. ed. (Lexington Books/Macmillan, 1993).

Weiland, Barbara, and Leslie Wood. *Clothes Sense: Straight Talking About Wardrobe Planning* (Palmer/Pletsch, 1984).

Whirlpool Laundry Guide, *Automatic Washers* (Whirlpool Corp., 1988).

Wood, Robert S. *Pleasure Packing* (Ten Speed Press, 1992).

Zepatos, Thalia. *A Journey of One's Own: Uncommon Advice for the Independent Woman Traveler* (The Eighth Mountain Press, 1992).